What You Can Do About EBOLA

CONTEMPORARY DISEASES AND DISORDERS

What You Can Do About
EBOLA

Edward Willett

Enslow Publishing
101 W. 23rd Street
Suite 240
New York, NY 10011
USA
enslow.com

Published in 2016 by Enslow Publishing, LLC
101 W. 23rd Street, Suite 240, New York, NY 10011

Cataloging-in-Publication Data

Willett, Edward.
  What you can do about ebola / by Edward Willett.
     p. cm. —(Contemporary diseases and disorders)
  Includes bibliographical references and index.
  ISBN 978-0-7660-7036-3 (library binding)
  1. Ebola virus disease — Juvenile literature. I. Willett, Edward, 1959–   . II. Title.
  RC140.5 W554 2016
  616.9'25—d23

Printed in the United States of America

To Our Readers: We have done our best to make sure all Web site addresses in this book were active and appropriate when we went to press. However, the author and the publisher have no control over and assume no liability for the material available on those Web sites or on any Web sites they may link to. Any comments or suggestions can be sent by e-mail to customerservice@enslow.com.

Portions of this book originally appeared in the book *Ebola Virus*.

CONTENTS

EBOLA AT A GLANCE

WHAT IS IT?

Ebola virus disease, previously known as Ebola hemorrhagic fever, is a rare and deadly disease caused by infection with one of the five known strains of Ebola virus. Historically it has been fatal in between 25 to 90 percent of cases, depending on the strain.

WHO GETS IT?

Ebola affects men and women of any age. It also infects nonhuman primates (monkeys, gorillas, and chimpanzees). Ebola virus is present in several African countries, where outbreaks occur sporadically.

HOW DO YOU GET IT?

The virus is introduced into the human population through close contact with the blood, secretions, organs or other bodily fluids of infected animals such as fruit bats, chimpanzees, gorillas, monkeys, forest antelope and porcupines found ill or dead or in the rain forest. Once a human is infected, the virus can be transmitted to other humans through direct contact (via broken skin or mucous membranes) with the bodily fluids of the infected person, or through contact with objects that have been contaminated with infected bodily fluids.

WHAT ARE THE SYMPTOMS?

The symptoms of Ebola vary from patient to patient, making it difficult to diagnose in the early stages. Most patients, within a few days of becoming infected, develop a sudden fever and may experience weakness, muscle pain, headaches and a sore throat. This may be followed by vomiting, diarrhea, and impaired kidney and liver function. Fewer than half of patients develop hemorrhagic symptoms, such as nosebleeds, bloody vomit, bloody diarrhea, internal bleeding, and conjunctivitis.

HOW IS IT TREATED?

No specific treatment or vaccine for Ebola has so far proved effective in humans, although several experimental drugs and vaccines are being studied. The best doctors can do is what's called "supportive therapy": treating the symptoms by balancing patients' fluids and electrolytes, making sure that they are getting enough oxygen, keeping up their blood pressure, providing high-quality nutrition, and treating any secondary infections with antibiotics.

HOW CAN IT BE PREVENTED?

Because Ebola outbreaks are thought to begin when humans come in contact with diseased animals, efforts to reduce the risk of Ebola include urging people who live in countries where the virus occurs naturally to take care when handling dead animals—using gloves and other protective clothing—and cooking meat thoroughly before consumption. Once an outbreak has begun, the key to preventing its spread is to limit contact with the bodily fluids of those infected. Those caring for ill patients at home should wear gloves and protective clothing. Regular hand washing after visiting patients in the hospital or caring for them at home is also important. Other steps include the prompt and safe burial of the dead, identifying everyone who has come in contact with those infected and monitoring them for twenty-one days (the time frame during which symptoms will appear), separating the sick from the healthy, good hygiene, and a clean environment.

Chapter 1

Four Decades of Terror

Ebola has become so much a part of public consciousness and concern that it's hard to believe its existence has only been known for forty years.

Its story begins in 1976 in the village of Yambuku in the Democratic Republic of the Congo, which in those days was still known as Zaire. Yambuku, located in the tropical rain forest about 100 miles (161 kilometers) south of the Ebola River, was home to the Yambuku Mission Hospital, which in 1976 served a population of some sixty thousand people.

Staffed by Catholic nuns, nurses and midwives, Yambuku Mission Hospital was a collection of small, tin-roofed huts with concrete floors, housing a pharmacy, an operating room, and 120 beds. It had no electricity and a shortage of basic medical supplies.

Nearly four hundred patients a day came through the hospital's outpatient clinic. The most common treatment was an injection of antibiotic. Unfortunately, the hospital did not have four hundred needles a day to use. It only had a dozen or so, so the nuns used the same needles over and over. In addition, the

The first known modern-day Ebola outbreak was in the village of Yambuku in Zaire, Africa. Zaire is now called the Democratic Republic of the Congo.

needles were not sterilized between injections. Instead, the nuns would just swish them around in a pan of warm water.

There had never been a major problem with this way of doing things in the forty-one years the hospital had been in operation. That changed in 1976, when Mabalo Lokela, a teacher at the Yambuku Mission School, came to the clinic suffering from a fever and other symptoms that the nurses diagnosed as malaria.

The usual treatment for malaria was a shot of chloroquine. The shot was given and Lokela was sent home. He felt better for a little while, but soon felt worse than ever. The next time he went to the hospital, he was admitted, suffering from high fever, bloody diarrhea, headache, chest pains, and nausea. He died three days later.

Lokela was only the first. The disease he carried, which had never been seen before, killed eighteen of his family and friends. Hundreds of other people were infected when they were injected using the same needles used on him. While some people who only touched him survived, no one who contracted the disease as a result of an injection did.[1] Eventually, 280 people died from a new and terrifying disease that became known as Ebola hemorrhagic fever[2], but is now called Ebola virus disease—or just Ebola, for short.

MOST DANGEROUS DISEASE OF ALL?

Thanks to a bestselling book by Richard Preston called *The Hot Zone*, about an outbreak of Ebola among monkeys at a US research facility, and a movie a few years later called *Outbreak*, about the fictional emergence of an airborne version of Ebola in the United States, there's a popular perception that Ebola is one of the most dangerous diseases known to man. It both is and is not. It *is* dangerous because its most virulent strain, Ebola-Zaire, kills up to nine out of ten people infected. However, it is *not* as dangerous as many people think because it is relatively hard to catch and risk factors are easily controlled. Unlike, say, influenza, which has killed millions of people over the years despite only killing a small percentage of the people who get it, the strains of Ebola that cause disease in humans apparently are not transmitted through the air, and even the most recent epidemic has killed far fewer people than influenza, meningitis, and many other infectious diseases kill every year.

Ebola is not normally present in humans. Instead, humans appear to come into contact with it by accident. That means there must be a "natural reservoir" of the virus—some animal or insect that carries it all the time and occasionally transmits it to a human. This natural reservoir hasn't been positively identified, but based on the evidence (and the nature of similar viruses), scientists think it's most likely fruit bats.[3]

There must be a "natural reservoir" of the virus— some animal or insect that carries it all the time and occasionally transmits it to a human.

Once a human has the disease, other humans can be infected by direct contact with the blood or other bodily secretions (sweat, saliva, etc.) of the infected person. People have also been infected with Ebola through contact with objects, especially hypodermic needles, which have been in contact with infected bodily secretions.

This means that the most common avenues of transmission of the disease during an outbreak are from one family member to another (because family members care for each other, and thus come in contact with bodily fluids) or among patients, doctors and nurses in hospitals, especially hospitals where needles and syringes are reused.[4] (The transmission of disease inside a hospital is called nosocomial transmission.)

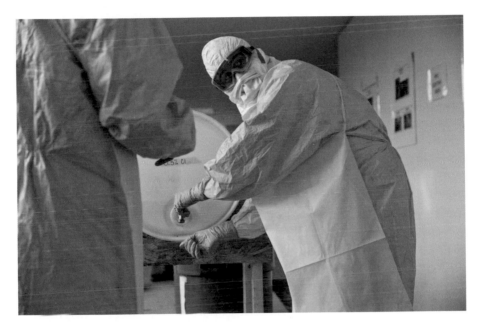

Proper precautions are crucial in stopping an outbreak of Ebola. These workers are wearing protective gowns, gloves, and masks and are sanitizing their hands after a simulated training session on how to care for Ebola patients.

The fact that Ebola is transmitted primarily by close contact with bodily fluids, however, also means that breaking the chain of transmission is relatively easy. Family members and friends of infected people and medical personnel must take basic precautions that prevent contact with bodily fluids, such as wearing masks, gloves, gowns, and goggles when caring for or treating an infected person. The patient should be isolated from all uninfected, nonmedical people. Finally, everything that comes in contact with the patient should be thoroughly sterilized.

While preventing further transmission of the disease is fairly simple, there are no effective treatments for those who are infected. Instead, patients receive therapy designed to treat the symptoms and prevent fatal shock. Because there is no effective treatment, efforts to battle Ebola outbreaks focus on breaking the chain of transmission. Preventing a single case from developing into a major outbreak depends on the disease being recognized early so proper safety precautions can be taken. That is difficult because, as was noted earlier, Ebola looks so much like so many other diseases in the early stages.

EBOLA IN THE UNITED STATES

Because of Ebola's reputation as a highly infectious, unstoppable killer disease (although, as has already been mentioned, it is neither all that infectious nor all that unstoppable), many people worry about the possibility of someone infected with Ebola traveling to another country, such as the United States, and starting an outbreak there.

As of this writing, there have been four confirmed cases of Ebola in the United States, all related to the epidemic in West Africa.

On September 30, 2014, the Centers for Disease Control (CDC) confirmed the United States's first case of Ebola: a man who had traveled to Dallas, Texas, from Liberia. He didn't have

Nina Pham, one of the Texas nurses who tested positive for Ebola after caring for a patient with the disease, is released from the NIH Clinical Center on October 24, 2014. Next to her is the director of the National Institute of Allergy and Infectious Diseases, Dr. Anthony Fauci.

symptoms when he left the African country, but developed them about four days after arriving in the United States. He was isolated at Texas Presbyterian Hospital of Dallas. Tests at the CDC and at a Texas laboratory confirmed he had Ebola. He died on October 28. All close contacts were monitored daily for twenty-one days; all completed the monitoring period without developing the disease.

However, on October 10, 2014, a healthcare worker at Texas Presbyterian Hospital who had provided care to the deceased patient tested positive for Ebola. She was isolated after reporting a fever, and was moved to the National Institutes of Health (NIH) Clinical Center, where she recovered. She was discharged on October 24.

On October 15, 2014, a second healthcare worker who had helped care for the initial patient tested positive for Ebola. She was transferred to Emory Hospital in Atlanta, Georgia.

Because she had traveled by air from Dallas to Cleveland on October 10 and from Cleveland to Dallas on October 13, the CDC had public health professionals contact all passengers and crew on the two flights. The patient recovered and was discharged on October 28, and all passengers on the two flights passed the twenty-one-day monitoring period without incident.

On October 23, 2014, the New York City Department of Health and Mental Hygiene reported a case of Ebola in a medical aid worker who had returned to New York City from Guinea. The patient recovered and was discharged from the hospital on November 11.[5]

So Ebola has already traveled to North America: thus far, it hasn't made any inroads into the general population. Still, it's such a frightening disease that people are understandably worried. To decide whether you *should* be worried, you need to understand what Ebola is, what it does, how it is transmitted, how it can be prevented, and what the prospects are for developing an effective treatment for it.

You will learn all that and more in the next few chapters.

Chapter 2

EBOLA: A BRIEF HISTORY

E bola was first identified in 1976, but obviously it's been around for a lot longer than that. In fact, some historians have even suggested that a plague that swept the eastern Mediterranean in the fifth century BC—a plague that helped bring about the end of the Golden Age of Greece—may in fact have been Ebola. Described in detail by historian and philosopher Thucydides, the plague struck Athens three times, in 430, 429, and 427–426 BC, at the height of the Pelopennesian War between Sparta and Athens.

At the time, Athens was much more crowded than usual because all the people from the outlying countryside had been brought into the city to protect them from attack by the Spartans. The plague killed large numbers of people, possibly including Pericles, leader of the Athenians; it has been estimated that between a quarter and a third of the population died.[1]

Thucydides, who contracted the disease but survived, said it originated in Ethiopia and spread through Egypt and Libya before falling on Athens. He said the symptoms included fever and redness and burning of the eyes, and that the inside of the

Ancient Greek historian Thucydides was the first to describe a disease that resembled Ebola in the 400s BC.

mouth turned bloody looking. He also said that the breath turned foul smelling and that after that came sneezing, hoarseness, coughing, bilious vomiting, and an "empty heaving." The flesh turned red and livid and broke out in blisters and ulcers. Victims suffered from unquenchable thirst and high fevers. Most died on the seventh or ninth day. Others died later of weakness after extreme diarrhea. Anyone who cared for the sick or even visited them caught the disease, Thucydides wrote.[2]

Many of those symptoms also plague modern Ebola victims. The "empty heaving" sounds odd, but it is possible that the Greek phrase could also be translated as "hiccups"—and 15 percent of Ebola patients in the outbreak of Ebola in Kikwit, Democratic Republic of the Congo, in 1995 also suffered from hiccups.[3]

So, was the Plague of Athens the first recorded outbreak of Ebola? Recent evidence seems to point instead to no. While Ebola may be one possibility, other theories have included bubonic plague, dengue fever, influenza, and measles. A recent study of DNA recovered from tooth pulp from victims of the disease strongly suggests typhoid fever was the more probable cause.[4]

EBOLA IN THE TWENTIETH CENTURY

Whether or not accounts of Ebola outbreaks are hidden among the records of historical plagues, we know for certain that the first outbreak of Ebola in modern times took place in Yambuku, a village in the tropical rain forests of the northern part of the Democratic Republic of the Congo (then called Zaire), in 1976.

The outbreak began when the teacher at the Yambuku Mission School came to the Yambuku Mission Hospital suffering from an illness that was first diagnosed as malaria. Soon that teacher was dead and hundreds more were infected due to unsterilized syringes. The death toll of 280 was 88 percent of the 318 cases reported.[5]

No one knew at first what was killing people. The hospital closed on September 30, 1976, just twenty-nine days after the teacher received his injection. By that time, eleven of the seventeen staff members had the mysterious disease. On October 18, 1976, the World Health Organization (WHO) formed an international commission to investigate. Research teams were mobilized on October 30, but by that time, the outbreak had burned itself out. The last case died on November 5.[6] Ironically, because most of the infections took place within the hospital, closing the hospital played the largest role in ending the outbreak.[7]

"WE HAD NO CLUE WHAT HAD CAUSED IT"

Although the outbreak took place in Yambuku, the realization that its victims were suffering from a previously unknown disease took place thousands of miles away in Belgium. Dr. Peter Piot was training in microbiology at the time at the Institute for Tropical Medicine in Antwerp. Dr. Piot and his colleagues received samples of liver tissue and blood from a nun who had worked, and died, at Yambuku Mission Hospital. As Dr. Piot described it:

> The diagnosis was yellow fever, but when we grew a culture we saw it was very different from yellow fever virus. The Centers for Disease Control and Prevention in Atlanta confirmed that the virus was unlike anything that had ever been documented. The next day I caught a plane to Zaire to join an international team that was investigating the outbreak. We had no clue to what had caused it.[8]

One of the people at the Centers for Disease Control and Prevention (CDC) who confirmed that the virus was unknown was Dr. Frederick A. Murphy. When Dr. Murphy put a sample from Zaire in an electron microscope on October 13, 1976, he

Dr. Peter Piot is a microbiologist who helped discover the Ebola virus in 1976. He went on to become a leading AIDS researcher.

expected to see the Marburg virus—and that is what he thought he saw. After disinfecting the room in which he had prepared the specimen, he shot photographs. According to Dr. Murphy:

> I went back to the microscope and called Karl Johnson and Patricia Webb to take a look. I shot a cassette of pictures with wet negatives not good for the enlarger and I made prints, which were available within minutes. I carried these dripping prints to the office of the Director of the CDC. It was very dramatic. [9]

The photographs revealed that in fact the virus was not Marburg, but something entirely new.

The new virus was called Ebola, after the little river 100 miles (161 kilometers) north of Yambuku; but in fact, the outbreak there was not the only one underway.

TWO STRAINS AT ONCE

Ebola also broke out in the towns of Nzara and Maridi and the surrounding area in Sudan in 1976—in fact, that outbreak actually occurred *before* the one in Yambuku. On June 27, 1976, a worker in the Nzara Cotton Manufacturing Factory cloth room became ill; he died in the Nzara hospital on July 6, 1976. A second man who worked in the cloth room died in the hospital on July 14; a third man became ill on July 18 and died on July 27, after several short stays in the hospital. He, in turn, appears to have infected many others—69 percent of the cases in the resulting outbreak were traced back to him.[10] In all, 284 cases were eventually identified. However, the strain of Ebola virus causing those cases turned out to be different from the one in Yambuku, and not quite as deadly. The death rate was 53 percent instead of 88 percent. Once again, the disease was spread mainly inside the hospital.[11] Ebola-Sudan, as this strain of the disease was dubbed, popped up again in Nzara in 1979. Thirty-four people became ill; twenty-two of them died. Once

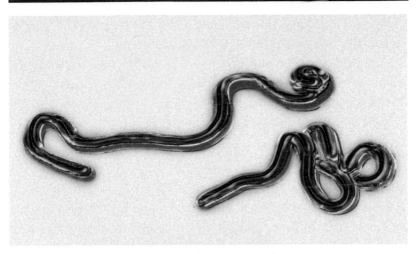

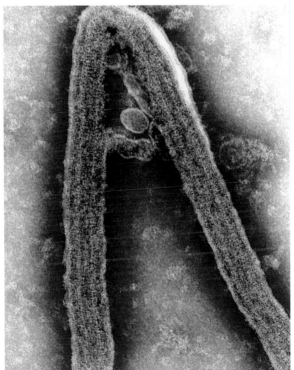

The Ebola (top) and Marburg (bottom) viruses cause illnesses that have similar symptoms, and they both come from the viral family *Filoviridae*.

again, every case could be connected back to someone employed at the Nzara Cotton Manufacturing Factory.[12]

No one was able to learn much about Ebola hemorrhagic fever during the first few outbreaks. Efforts were made to find the "reservoir species"—it was presumed that animals carried the virus in the wild—but without success.

THE HOT ZONE

The next time Ebola surfaced, it was not in Africa. Instead, it showed up in the United States in monkeys imported from the Philippines. This outbreak, first discovered at Hazleton Research Products' Reston Primate Quarantine Unit in Reston, Virginia, became famous as the subject of the book *The Hot Zone*. One hundred cynomolgus macaques from Ferlite Farms in Mindanao, Philippines, were quarantined in Reston on October 4, 1989. (United States law requires all primates imported into the country to be quarantined for thirty days, to ensure that they are free of disease.) All one hundred monkeys were placed in the same room, Room F.

Any transcontinental shipment of animals tends to result in a number of deaths, but many more of the monkeys in this shipment died than would ordinarily have been expected. The staff veterinarian examined some of the dead monkeys and concluded they had died of a disease called simian hemorrhagic fever (SHF), which is similar to Ebola but does not infect humans.

However, he sent samples of the tissue to the United States Army Medical Research Institute of Infectious Diseases (USAMRIID) and euthanized all of the monkeys in Room F to prevent the possible spread of the disease. USAMRIID confirmed the presence of SHF in the samples, but euthanizing the monkeys did not solve the problem. More monkeys in a different room (Room H) died, and the disease no longer looked very much like SHF in the way it progressed or the way it spread. That was confirmed by USAMRIID, which, as it continued to examine the dead monkey tissue, eventually found the Ebola virus present in addition to SHF.[13]

The Room H monkeys had arrived in Reston on November 8, eight days before the Room F monkeys were euthanized. They had also come from Ferlite Farms in the Philippines, which, investigators later discovered, was experiencing a hemorrhagic fever outbreak at the same time. The question was, did the Room H monkeys catch the virus from the Room F monkeys (which would mean that the Ebola virus was transmitted through the air, rather than by close contact—something that would make it far more dangerous), or were they already harboring the virus, without showing symptoms, when they arrived?

In *The Hot Zone*, which influenced the public's view of Ebola as one of the world's most dangerous diseases, Richard Preston concluded that the virus was transmitted through the air. However, subsequent research seems to indicate that wasn't the case. A recent study showed no transmission of Ebola virus among nonhuman primates placed about a foot apart in separate open-barred cages and ambient air conditions, but with a Plexiglas divider that prevented direct contact between the animals.[14]

On November 29, the CDC and the Virginia Department of Health, along with USAMRIID, decided to euthanize all the remaining animals in Room H to prevent the disease from spreading to other monkeys in the facility and possibly to the human staff. On November 30, around five hundred monkeys were euthanized.

Tests of the staff revealed that four humans had developed antibodies to Ebola, indicating they had been infected, but none of them became ill. The strain infecting the monkeys appeared to be different from either Ebola-Zaire or Ebola-

Sudan, and apparently does not cause disease in humans. It was named Ebola-Reston.

Ebola-Reston turned up again in monkey quarantine facilities in the United States in Philadelphia (at about the same time as the outbreak in Reston) and in Texas (a couple of months later). All the monkeys involved came from the Ferlite Farms in the Philippines, but no human who was exposed to the virus, either there or in the United States, became ill.

TWO MORE STRAINS APPEAR

A fourth strain of Ebola surfaced in Taï Forest National Park in Côte d'Ivoire (Ivory Coast) in 1994. This time, the victims were members of a wild troop of chimpanzees being studied by scientists. In October and November of 1994, twelve members of the troop died. Autopsies of some of the dead chimps revealed damage to the internal organs similar to those of human victims of Ebola. The Pasteur Institute confirmed that diagnosis. Researchers noted that the deaths corresponded to a time when the chimpanzees were hunting and eating Western Red Colobus monkeys, and those who ate the most meat were the most likely to die. As a result, they suspected the monkeys were carrying the virus, which turned out to be a new strain of Ebola, originally called Ebola-Ivory Coast but now known as Ebola-Taï Forest.

Ebola-Taï Forest does cause disease in humans, but it may not be as deadly to humans as Ebola-Zaire and Ebola-Sudan. One of the scientists who autopsied one of the dead chimps became ill eight days later. She was transported to Switzerland for treatment, and recovered. No one else was infected, even though strict quarantine procedures were not followed.[15]

A fifth strain of Ebola was identified during an outbreak in the Bundibugyo district of western Uganda from August 2007 to February 2008. Ebola-Bundibugyo proved to be less fatal than the Zaire and Sudan strains, with a case fatality rate of 34

The Taï Forest in Ivory Coast, Africa, is the site where the fourth strain of Ebola was first discovered.

percent. Most of the disease transmission was associated with handling of dead bodies without appropriate protection.[16]

ZAIRE IS HIT AGAIN

By 1995, sixteen years had passed since there had been a major outbreak of Ebola affecting humans. Suddenly it surfaced again, once again in Zaire, once again in a hospital, once again with deadly effects. This time, the center of outbreak was Kikwit, a city of 500,000 people.[17]

On April 6, 1995, a thirty-six-year-old laboratory technician named Kimfumu, who worked at the Mama Mobutu Maternity Hospital, fell ill with a fever. Two days later, he was admitted to the hospital. Doctors originally thought he had typhoid. Then his stomach became distended, which made them think he had a perforated intestine, which required an immediate operation. They transferred him to Kikwit General Hospital, which had the facilities for operations, and on April 10, he was operated on by two doctors and two nurses. They removed his appendix and he seemed to get better, but then his stomach became even more bloated, and a second operation was performed. This time, they found that his abdominal cavity was filled with blood because his internal organs were leaking fluids and blood into it. The doctors and nurses were spattered with Kimfumu's blood. Kimfumu went into shock and died on April 14.

Soon, members of the operating team began dying, and news of an outbreak of Ebola in Zaire made it into the outside world.[18] Thanks to the popularity of *The Hot Zone* and other books, Ebola was a hot topic. The media flooded Kikwit. Television, newspapers, and magazines were filled with stories about the outbreak.

Scientists also poured into Kikwit. They found that the outbreak had actually begun long before Kimfumu became ill. The first case, or "index case," was a thirty-five-year-old charcoal maker and farmer named Gaspar Menga. He worked about eight to ten miles (thirteen to sixteen kilometers) from Kikwit in the Pont Mwembe forest. On January 6, 1995, he developed a fever, bloody diarrhea, and abdominal pain. He was diagnosed at Kikwit General Hospital with a fairly common abdominal disease in the region, caused by a bacterium called *Shigella*. But by January 13 he had died, and soon so had almost every member of his family.

Funerals in the region were traditionally open-casket, and it was also traditional for family members to put their hands on the body during funerals as a last gesture of affection and farewell. Menga's wife, Bebe, his brother, Bilolo, and his uncle, Philemond, all touched the body—and all were dead by the end of January.

That wave of deaths led to a second wave—sisters, sons, daughters, and grandmother—in February, then a third wave, culminating in the death of another grandmother on March 3 in an outlying village.[19]

For some reason, that part of the outbreak died out at that point; no more cases were reported from it. However, a friend of the Menga family was admitted to Mama Mobutu Maternity Hospital and died there on March 3. There were two other deaths there in March and, at the beginning of April, six more. Kimfumu probably caught the disease during his work as a laboratory technician; the other lab technician, Bienge, had actually entered the hospital the day before Kimfumu and died on the same day.[20]

Although he was not the true "patient zero" of the outbreak, Kimfumu was the one who brought the disease to Kikwit General Hospital. Just as in the first Ebola outbreak in 1976, the hospital became the focal point of the subsequent infections and deaths. Patients would enter the hospital and infect family members and hospital staff, who would then leave the hospital

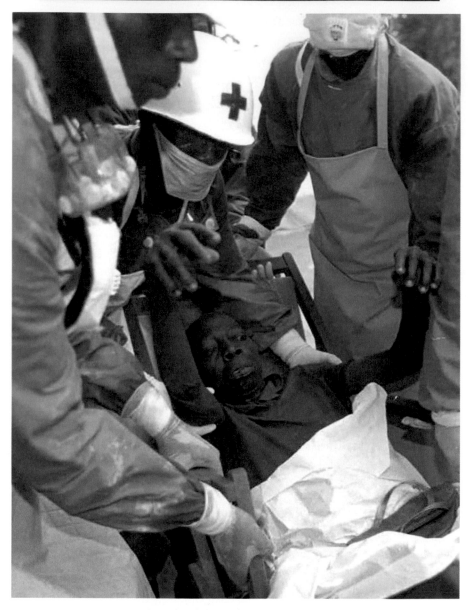

In 1995 a new outbreak of Ebola hit Zaire. Here, Red Cross workers help a patient who is suspected of being infected with the disease.

and infect other people, then return to the hospital as patients and continue the cycle.[21]

The CDC specialists who arrived on the scene to attempt to halt the outbreak had difficulty convincing infected people to come to the hospital, because it had become so closely associated in people's minds with death. Some people hid themselves away rather than be taken to the hospital.[22] That made stopping the outbreak much more difficult than it would otherwise have been, but eventually quarantining patients and proper safety procedures stopped the chain of transmission. The final tally of the outbreak was 315 confirmed human cases and 250 deaths— an 81 percent fatality rate.[23]

Patients would enter the hospital and infect family members and hospital staff, who would then leave the hospital and infect other people, then return to the hospital as patients and continue the cycle.

As in 1976, scientists searched the forest for the natural reservoir of the virus—and as in 1976, found nothing.

EBOLA STRIKES GABON

Three smaller outbreaks of Ebola-Zaire occurred in Gabon just before and after the Kikwit outbreak. The first, in 1994, attracted no attention at the time because it was initially thought to be yellow fever. Occurring in gold-mining camps deep in the rain forest, it infected fifty-two people, of whom thirty-one died, for a fatality rate of 60 percent.[24]

The "yellow fever" outbreak was determined to have been Ebola in 1995, the same year as the Kikwit outbreak in Zaire. A year later, in 1996, two more outbreaks occurred in Gabon. In the first, a chimpanzee found dead in the forest was butchered and eaten by a group of people out searching for food. Nineteen people who were involved in butchering the chimpanzee

A nun helps two healthcare workers in Zaire remove their surgical gloves after treating patients. Safety precautions like these protective gloves and gowns helped to eventually halt the progression of Ebola in the area.

became ill; the remaining eighteen cases in the outbreak were among their family members. Twenty-one people, or 57 percent of the cases, died.[25]

In the second outbreak, a hunter who lived in a forest camp became infected, and then spread the disease to others. In all, sixty people became infected and forty-five of them died. Interestingly, a chimpanzee may have also been involved in that outbreak; a dead chimp found in the forest was discovered to have been infected with Ebola. A medical professional who treated Ebola patients in Gabon became ill after traveling to Johannesburg, South Africa. He survived, but a nurse who took care of him in South Africa died. No one else was infected.[26]

ATTEMPTS TO UNDERSTAND THE DISEASE

After the Kikwit and Gabon outbreaks, researchers continued their efforts to discover how the Ebola virus carries out its gruesome work. In July 2000, researchers at the US National Institutes of Health (NIH) and the CDC, led by Dr. Gary Nabel of the NIH's Vaccine Research Center, identified the major gene in the Ebola virus that kills cells, and the protein produced by that gene that causes blood vessels to leak in an infected person. It was an important step toward eventually developing drugs to counteract Ebola—or a vaccine to prevent it.[27]

Just two months later, a new outbreak of Ebola began in Uganda. This time the strain was Ebola-Sudan. This outbreak was different in that Uganda had more modern hospital facilities than the Democratic Republic of the Congo. As a result, most of the transmission of the disease happened within the community rather than in the hospital (although many health workers died before proper safety procedures were put in place).

A particular problem in this outbreak was the local practice of family members ritually bathing each dead body, then

A hospital worker disinfects villagers in Gulu, Uganda, after they buried an Ebola victim in 2000.

washing their hands in a communal basin. As a result, many families were entirely wiped out by the virus.[28]

The outbreak might have been far worse if not for efforts by the Ugandan government to contain it. Approximately 5,600 people who had been in contact with patients were identified and kept under observation for twenty-one-day periods by 150 trained volunteers. Efforts to educate the public and local medical workers about the importance of proper safety procedures while dealing with victims of the disease were also important.[29]

Eventually, 425 cases of Ebola hemorrhagic fever were confirmed and 224 people died, a death rate of 53 percent.[30] Researchers once again began searching for the natural reservoir of the virus, without success.

Even while the Ugandan outbreak was still raging, more scientific advances were being made in the fight against Ebola. In November 2000, news appeared that researchers at the CDC had created a vaccine that prevented four macaque monkeys deliberately infected with Ebola from contracting the disease.[31]

Many more outbreaks of Ebola occurred over the next decade. All were brought under control fairly quickly, using lessons learned from the outbreaks of the 1990s.

That all changed in 2014.

FROM OUTBREAK TO EPIDEMIC

On December 26, 2013, in the village of Meliandou, Guinea, an eighteen-month-old boy named Emile Ouamouno developed a fever, black stools, and vomiting. Before he got sick, he'd been seen playing in his backyard near a hollow tree where bats lived.

By the second week of January 2014, several members of Emile's immediate family had also fallen ill, and soon died. So did several midwives, traditional healers, and staff at a hospital in the city of Gueckedou who treated them. More of the boy's extended family, who attended funerals or took care of ill relatives,

MAJOR EBOLA OUTBREAKS FROM 2001–2012

October 2001–March 2002
Gabon, Zaire virus—65 infected, 53 deaths (82 percent)

October 2001–March 2002
Republic of the Congo, Zaire virus—57 infected, 43 deaths (75 percent)

December 2002–April 2003
Republic of the Congo, Zaire virus—143 infected, 128 deaths (89 percent)

November–December 2003
Republic of the Congo, Zaire virus—35 infected, 29 deaths (83 percent)

2004
South Sudan, Sudan virus—17 infected, 7 deaths (41 percent),

2007
Democratic Republic of the Congo, Zaire virus—264 infected, 187 deaths (71 percent)

December 2007–January 2008
Uganda, Bundibugyo virus (first reported occurrence)— 149 infected, 37 deaths (25 percent)

December 2008–February 2009
Democratic Republic of the Congo, Zaire virus—32 infected, 15 deaths (47 percent)

2012
Uganda, Sudan virus—11 infected, 4 deaths (36.4 percent)

November 2012–January 2013
Uganda, Sudan virus—6 infected, 3 deaths (50 percent)

2012
Democratic Republic of the Congo, Bundibugyo virus—36 infected, 13 deaths (36.1 percent)

fell ill and died during the following week. The illness had spread to four subdistricts by then. The world's largest—and as of this writing, still ongoing—Ebola epidemic had begun.

Local health officials began investigating the outbreak on January 25, 2014, but didn't reach any firm conclusions: The symptoms, including diarrhea, vomiting, and severe dehydration, appeared similar to those of cholera, one of many infectious diseases widespread in the region.

A larger team, including staff from Médecins Sans Frontières (Doctors Without Borders) traveled to Meliandou on January 27. They discovered bacteria in samples from the patients, which supported the notion that the disease was likely cholera. More deaths occurred, but were neither reported nor investigated.

On February 1, an infected member of Emile's extended family carried the virus into the capital city, Conakry. He died four days later in the hospital. Having no reason to suspect Ebola, the doctors and staff took no protective measures. As February continued, more cases spread to many other villages and cities in the region.

Guinea's Ministry of Health issued its first alert on March 13, 2014. At the time, the disease was suspected to be Lassa fever. But on March 22, the Institut Pasteur in Lyon, France, confirmed the disease was the Ebola-Zaire virus, the most lethal of the five known species. On March 23 the WHO publicly announced the outbreak. At that time, forty-nine cases and twenty-nine deaths had been officially reported.[32]

As of June 9, 2015, there had been 27,272 total cases (suspected, probable, and confirmed), 15,058 laboratory-confirmed cases, and 11,173 deaths. Guinea, Liberia, and Sierra Leone had been hardest hit, although cases had also been reported in Nigeria, Senegal, Mali, Spain, the United States, and the United Kingdom.[33]

The scale of this epidemic shone a spotlight on Ebola research. It is safe to say we know more about the disease now than we ever have before, as you'll see in the next chapter.

Emile Ouamouno's father (second from the left) stands next to the mayor (third from left) of Meliandou as he informs village residents on how to protect themselves from Ebola. Emile's death marked the beginning of the worst Ebola epidemic in modern history.

Chapter 3

ANATOMY OF A DEADLY DISEASE

Before you can figure out how to combat a disease, you have to understand it. Here is what we know so far: Ebola virus disease is a severe, often-fatal disease that occurs in humans and nonhuman primates (monkeys and chimpanzees). It is caused by infection with Ebola virus, one of two members of a family of viruses called the *Filoviridae* because they look wormlike under the electron microscope. (*Filo* is Latin for "worm.") The other member of the family, Marburg virus, also causes a hemorrhagic fever (a disease characterized by both fever and uncontrolled bleeding).

Viruses are essentially just a bit of genetic material—RNA, in the case of Ebola—wrapped up inside a coat of protein. They are not, strictly speaking, alive, and they are incredibly tiny: A million viruses put together would be about the size of a speck of dust. However, the genetic material they carry inside is a code for making new copies of themselves.

Viruses, however, cannot replicate on their own. Instead, they take over the machinery of a living cell. Cells are essentially factories for turning out things like hormones, enzymes, and proteins. Viruses hijack these factories so that the cell, instead of producing what it is supposed to produce, turns out new copies of the virus. The process sometimes kills the cell; at the very least, it is bad news for the body the cell inhabits because the cell is no longer turning out the vital products it used to produce.[1]

Symptoms of Ebola may begin anywhere from two to twenty-one days after exposure. At first the disease may appear to be nothing more serious than influenza (the flu), with the initial symptoms typically consisting of sudden fever, chills, and a general feeling of illness; weakness; loss of appetite; severe headache; and back and body aches.

> **Symptoms of Ebola may begin anywhere from two to twenty-one days after exposure.**

However, a few days after the initial symptoms, other symptoms may develop, including watery diarrhea, nausea and vomiting, belly pain, and rash. Bleeding or bruising may also

A CHANGE IN NAME

In the past, Ebola and the other fever caused by a filovirus, Marburg, were classified as hemorrhagic fevers because the viruses sometimes prevent the blood from clotting properly, leading to uncontrolled bleeding.

However, more recently scientists have quit using the term "hemorrhagic fever" to refer to Ebola because only a small percentage of Ebola patients actually develop significant bleeding. When it does occur, it's usually late in the final phase of a terminal illness, when the patient is already in shock. In other words, the patient is already dying from the other effects of the virus before bleeding occurs, rather than the bleeding causing shock and death.[2]

develop, although it doesn't affect everyone. If it does happen, bleeding may reveal itself as tiny purple spots (caused by bursting blood vessels), bloody diarrhea or bowel movements, and blood oozing from the mouth, nose, eyes, or anywhere the skin has been broken.[3]

Not everyone who gets Ebola dies from it. The death rate in outbreaks has ranged from 25 percent to 90 percent. In the latter case, that means almost nine out of every ten patients who contracted Ebola died from it.

There are five species of Ebola virus, each named after the region where it was first identified: Zaire, Sudan, Ivory Coast/Taï Forest, Bundibugyo, and Reston.

Only four of the strains are known to cause disease in humans. The Zaire virus, since it was first recognized in 1976 in Yambuku, has caused many outbreaks in Central Africa, with death rates from 55 to 88 percent. This is the species that caused the massive epidemic in West Africa that began in 2014.

The Sudan virus has a mortality rate of approximately 50 percent. It has caused four outbreaks so far: three in Sudan, two in the 1970s and one in 2004, and one in Uganda in 2000.

The Taï Forest (formerly Ivory Coast) virus, has only caused illness in one person that we know of, and that person survived. The patient was a scientist studying a chimpanzee found dead in the forest, where the great ape population had greatly decreased.

The Bundibugyo virus was first identified in Uganda in 2007, when it caused an outbreak with a mortality rate of around 30 percent, much lower than the Zaire and Sudan viruses typically cause. It's closely related to the Taï Forest species.

The Reston virus, unlike all the others, has not been found in Africa; instead, it seems to originate in the Philippines. In 1989 it killed several macaques from the Philippines at a research facility in Reston, Virginia. Three more outbreaks

Healthcare workers in Guinea transport a patient suspected of having Ebola in 2014. The recent outbreak in West Africa is Ebola-Zaire, the most deadly strain.

occurred among nonhuman primates in the United States and Europe, all linked to the same Philippine animal supplier. No humans exposed to the sick animals became ill, although some developed antibodies to the virus, indicating they'd been infected.

In 2008 the Reston virus unexpectedly showed up during the investigation of an outbreak of illness in pigs in the Philippines. Some of the animals were infected both by an arterivirus (a porcine reproductive and respiratory disease virus) and by Ebola-Reston. Some Philippine pig farmers were found to carry antibodies to Ebola-Reston, but never developed severe symptoms. This seems to indicate Ebola-Reston can infect humans, but only causes mild symptoms or no symptoms at all.[4]

Ebola is believed to circulate naturally within animals in the wild, although the precise species of animals that serve as the "reservoir species" has not been positively identified. However, fruit bats are seen as among the most likely hosts.

Scientists believe that in outbreaks, the first patient becomes infected through contact with an infected animal, such as a fruit bat or nonhuman primate. This is called a "spillover event." Person-to-person transmission follows and can lead to large numbers of affected people.[5]

Once the virus makes the jump from its unknown animal host into humans, humans can spread it to other humans in several ways. The most common method is through direct contact with the blood or other bodily secretions (sweat, saliva, vomit, etc.) of an infected person. That is why outbreaks often wipe out whole families who live in close quarters and care for each other when they are sick. People can also be exposed to Ebola virus through contact with contaminated objects, especially hypodermic needles.

Ebola is not spread through the air or water or, in general, food (although in Africa it may be spread by handling the meat

Scientists have not yet been able to pinpoint the host, or reservoir, species responsible for carrying Ebola. Fruit bats are on the list of likely suspects.

of wild animals who were infected). There is no evidence mosquitoes or other insects can transmit Ebola virus.[6]

Since the publication of *The Hot Zone* and the release of the movie *Outbreak,* there has been concern that Ebola might mutate to become transmissible by air. However, scientists believe this is unlikely. Ebola is an ancient virus that split off from other viruses dating back thousands of years, and since being discovered has proved to be very stable, with a relatively constant mutation rate: The Ebola virus samples from the West African epidemic are 97 percent similar to the virus that emerged in 1976.

Most mutations have no effect on the virus at all, and for Ebola to become airborne would require multiple mutations over a very long period of time. Scientists monitoring the virus have seen no indication those kinds of mutations are occurring.[7]

SYMPTOMS OF EBOLA VIRUS DISEASE

One of the most insidious things about Ebola virus disease, as with many deadly illnesses, is that at its start it does not seem very serious.

Ebola symptoms begin with fever, chills, headaches, muscle aches, and loss of appetite, usually within one to two weeks after infection. Because these symptoms also mimic those of other tropical infections such as salmonellosis, typhoid fever, yellow fever, viral hepatitis, malaria, and others, Ebola is often misdiagnosed in the early stages, increasing the risk of the disease being passed on to others within a healthcare setting.

By day five to seven of the illness, a rash may develop on the face, neck, trunk and arms. Gastrointestinal symptoms such as watery diarrhea, nausea, vomiting, and abdominal pain are common, and can result in severe fluid loss. Despite the popular perception of Ebola as a disease involving uncontrolled bleeding, major bleeding is not particularly common. In the

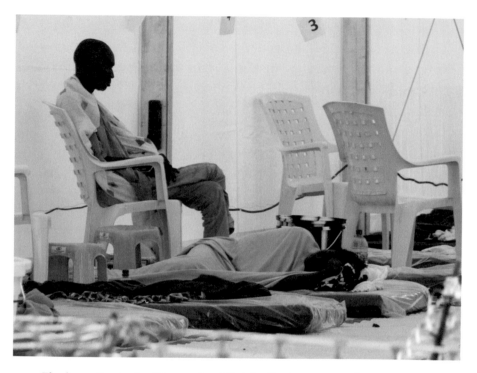

Ebola patients in Monrovia, Liberia. Patients are often misdiagnosed during the early stages of the disease because it resembles many other common illnesses.

West African epidemic, only about 20 percent of patients have unexplained hemorrhage. Blood in the stool is the most common manifestation of this (about six percent of this), although it can also manifest as purple spots on the skin, bruising, oozing from IV and injection punctures, or bleeding from mucous membranes. Major bleeding is most commonly seen in patients near death.

After about day ten, some patients develop symptoms like an altered state of consciousness, a stiff neck, and/or seizures. Ebola patients may also develop hiccups, chest pain, and/or shortness of breath. Their eyes may appear red, and the soft palate—the soft tissue at the back of the root of the mouth—is often discolored, turning dark red. Pregnant women may experience miscarriages.[8]

A BAD SIGN

In the popular imagination, Ebola victims almost literally melt away, blood pouring out of them; but as noted, that's not necessarily the case. What *is* the case is that bleeding, when it does occur, is a very bad sign.

Philippe Calain and Pierre Rollin were two of the doctors from the CDC who were sent to Kikwit, Zaire, at the time of the 1995 outbreak of Ebola. In the General Hospital, they found and spoke to many patients suffering from the disease.

"Most of the time they said they were thirsty," Calain said. He continued:

> Not mainly because they had nothing to drink, but
> because one of the symptoms of the disease is a very sore
> throat and pain in swallowing. That was one of their main
> complaints—that and extreme weakness, weakness that
> you suffer of. It is difficult to imagine lying on a bed and
> suffering from being weak. Even lifting their head was a big,
> huge effort.[9]

Rollin agreed:

> They all were very tired. Some say that they had headache,
> chest pain, back pain. Most of them do not want to talk,
> they are too exhausted to talk. They do not want to do
> anything, they just want to die. That is one of the signs of
> Ebola: people are really very exhausted, the whole time.[10]

Something else the patients had in common was a fixed, upward stare. Their faces were expressionless masks.

Calain continued:

> At the end of the disease the patient does not look, from the
> outside, as horrible as you can read in some books: they are
> not 'melting,' they are not full of blood. They are in shock,
> muscular shock. They are not unconscious, but you would
> say 'obtunded'—dull, quiet, very tired.[11]

Despite Ebola's reputation, "Very few were hemorrhaging; hemorrhage is not the main symptom," Rollin said. "Less than half of the patients had some kind of hemorrhage."

But, he added, "the ones that bled, died."[12]

Chapter 4

IS IT EBOLA?

A s the history of Ebola in Chapter 2 explains, quite often when Ebola makes an appearance, no one is sure what it is. Because it shares initial symptoms with many other diseases that are endemic in tropical countries, it's easy for it to get a foothold while doctors are still, in effect, looking the other way.

When Ebola reappeared in Kikwit General Hospital in 1995, no one knew at first what it was. Tamfum Muyembe, a virologist from the University of Kinshasa, was called in to assess the situation. He had been at the original Ebola outbreak in Yambuku in 1976, and so was familiar with the disease.

Muyembe arrived in Kikwit on May 1, 1995, learned what was known about the outbreak so far, and correctly deduced that a viral hemorrhagic fever of some sort was to blame. However, the only way to be sure that it was Ebola was to send blood samples to a qualified lab, one with the capability to work safely with the world's most dangerous diseases. Such labs are rare—and there was no such lab in Zaire.

After a break of almost twenty years, the second major outbreak of Ebola in humans began here in 1995 at Kikwit General Hospital in Zaire.

Instead, Muyembe had a military nurse draw blood from fourteen patients on May 4 and 5. Then he placed the samples in a metal canister, stuffed cotton wadding around the tubes, put the canister in a plastic box, and filled the box with ice. His plan was to send the samples to the Institute of Tropical Medicine in Antwerp, Belgium.

Muyembe gave the samples to the French deputy bishop, along with a diagram, "Relationship among cases at Kikwit," that showed the probable path the disease had taken from victim to victim, and a letter for Dr. Jean-Pierre Lahaye at the Belgian embassy in Kinshasa, Zaire.

The deputy bishop flew to Kinshasa on May 5. He delivered the samples to Dr. Lahaye, who read Muyembe's letter. The letter directed him to open the box, renew the ice, and then forward the samples to Belgium.

Going through proper channels to get the samples out of Zaire and into Belgium would have taken hours or even days. Because of the urgency, the samples were instead sent with a Zairian woman who made frequent business trips to Belgium. She took them on the plane as carry-on luggage.[1] She delivered them to Dr. Johan van Mullem, who worked at the Brussels headquarters of the Belgian Development Cooperation. It was the weekend and his office was closed, so he took the samples home with him.

The next morning, he called Simon Van Nieuwenhove, a colleague of his who was in charge of the medical projects funded by the Central Africa Service of their agency, and who was familiar with Ebola, having been at both the Yambuku and Sudan outbreaks in 1976. Van Nieuwenhove picked up the samples and drove them to Antwerp to deliver them to Professor Guido van der Groen.

Back in 1976, van der Groen's lab had received the first specimens from Yambuku and had tested them. He had been the first person to see the virus under the electron microscope

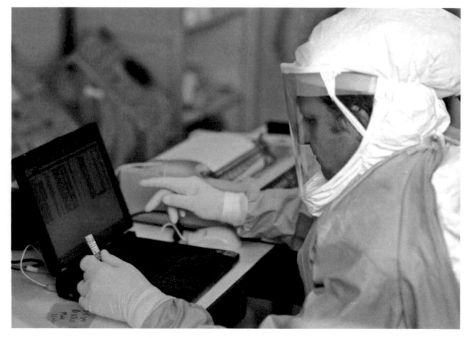

Pierre Rollin of the CDC tests blood samples for the Ebola virus.

and had taken the first photograph of it.[2] "This time I could not do anything with them," he said. "I no longer had the proper biosafety lab, I no longer had the diagnostic tools to make a rapid diagnosis, and so I had to send them on to the CDC."[3]

He took the samples to his lab, opened the box to make sure the samples were not leaking, and then froze everything. With difficulty, he eventually located some dry ice to pack into the box, found the Federal Express office, and convinced the clerk to accept the box for shipment, "by looking in a convincing way into the charming eyes of the young lady."[4]

The samples finally made it to the CDC in Atlanta on Tuesday, May 9, where Tom Ksiazek, laboratory chief of the Special Pathogens Branch, received them. He and Pierre Rollin, chief of the pathogenesis section, put on surgical gowns and gloves and took the box into the Level 3 Biosafety Lab. There, they opened the outer cardboard box. Inside that was a Styrofoam shipper, and inside that, packed in dry ice, was the metal canister that contained, in Ziploc plastic bags, frozen vials of whole blood.

The information on the vials, which indicated what patient the blood was from and when it was drawn, was entered into the computer. Then, Rollin climbed into a "space suit"—a suit that completely encases the wearer in plastic and has its own air supply separate from the air supply in the room—and went through an air lock into the Level 4 Biosafety Lab, which is completely sealed away from the outside world so that nothing can escape from it.

Rollin first defrosted the samples, then divided them into smaller portions. He set some of the portions to one side, and then irradiated the rest with gamma rays to kill any virus they contained, so he could work with the samples outside of the Level 4 lab.

He took the irradiated samples out of the Level 4 lab into a Level 3 lab and handed them over to Mary Lane Martin, a

LEVELS OF BIOSAFETY

Biosafety levels describe the types of measures in place in a laboratory to prevent the accidental escape of the bacteria or viruses being worked with there.

There are four levels of biosafety:

- *Biosafety Level 1 labs are for working with microorganisms not known to cause disease in healthy human adults. No special protective measures are involved, other than a sink for hand washing.*

- *Biosafety Level 2 labs are for working with microorganisms that do cause disease, but can be worked with safely on an open bench, provided there is little risk of splashing or spraying. Splash shields, face protection equipment, gowns and gloves, and closed cabinets are used as required.*

- *Biosafety Level 3 labs are for working with microorganisms that could be transmitted through respiration and can cause serious and potentially lethal infections (tuberculosis bacteria is one example). In Level 3 labs, all manipulation of samples is done inside a closed, airtight cabinet. Level 3 labs usually have controlled access and their own ventilation system to prevent the escape of infectious airborne particles.*

- *Biosafety Level 4 labs are for working with dangerous and exotic agents that pose a high individual risk of life-threatening disease, which may be transmitted via the air, and for which there is no available vaccine or therapy (Ebola, for example). In Level 4 labs, all workers wear "spacesuits" with an air supply from outside the lab. The lab has its own ventilation system and neither air nor waste materials are released without first being thoroughly decontaminated.*

Researchers get ready to work in a Biosafety Level 4 lab. These labs handle the most deadly viruses, like Ebola.

research microbiologist. It was she, days after the samples were taken and thousands of miles from the site of the outbreak, who finally made the diagnosis: The patients in Kikwit were indeed infected with the Ebola virus.[5]

> *It's important to diagnose the disease quickly in order to limit its spread—and yet, perversely, Ebola is very difficult to diagnose quickly.*

As was pointed out in the last chapter, Ebola looks very much like many other tropical diseases during its early stages. It's important to diagnose the disease quickly in order to limit its spread—and yet, perversely, Ebola is very difficult to diagnose quickly. The virus can only be detected in blood after the onset of symptoms, most notably fever, which is the body's reaction to the increasing volume of the virus circulating within it. Even after symptoms start, it may take up to three days for the virus to reach detectable levels.[6]

THE ELISA TEST

One method of diagnosis is called the ELISA (enzyme-linked immunosorbent assay) test. This was the method Mary Lane Martin used on the samples from Kikwit. She first took a prepared plastic plate, then placed measured amounts of the samples into the ninety-six wells that dimpled the plate. Then she conducted an ELISA test. These tests are the standard procedure for identifying unknown viruses. A sample of the unknown virus is added to an enzyme that reacts chemically to only one specific virus. In the presence of the right virus, the enzyme turns a specific color (green, in the case of the test for Ebola virus). Once one of the enzymes turns color, it is clear what virus has been identified.

The actual procedure is a bit more complicated. Various reagents have to be deposited in the right order, washed off

An ELISA test, similar to the one shown here, was conducted to identify the Ebola virus at the onset of the 1995 outbreak. Each well contains a sample, which is added to an enzyme. If a virus is present, the enzyme will change color.

again, then mixed with something else, and sometimes incubated. It took Martin about three hours to actually get the samples to the point where she could add the last reagent—the one that would turn green if Ebola virus were present.

"I could see immediately when I added the last reagent that it was going to be positive," Martin said. "It started the color change almost immediately. I knew right away that they were going to be positive."[7]

ISOLATING THE VIRUS

The ELISA test is not the only way to diagnose Ebola. Another method is to grow any viruses that are in a blood sample in a culture. But this has its own problems, as another story shows.

On November 6, 1996, nurse Marilyn Lahana was admitted to the Sandton Clinic, north of Johannesburg, South Africa, complaining of a severe headache, diarrhea, loss of appetite, and a high temperature. She was tested for malaria, meningitis, typhoid, and many other diseases, but test results showed she not have any of them.

However, Dr. Reeve Jobson, who was caring for Lahana, knew that there had recently been an outbreak of Congo fever, a type of viral hemorrhagic fever less virulent than Ebola, and suspected that might be Lahana's illness. On November 9, he sent ten milliliters of Lahana's blood to South Africa's National Institute for Virology, asking them to test the blood for viral hemorrhagic fevers.

The first test was to check for antibodies to various viral hemorrhagic fevers. Nothing turned up, so Jobson decided that he had been wrong and Lahana probably did not have a viral hemorrhagic fever. However, this test, which can be carried out fairly quickly, only turns up positive results later in the course of the disease or in the blood of patients who recover. For that reason, the laboratory also began to grow culture of the viruses found in Lahana's blood. Once enough viruses have been grown, they can be identified.

Unfortunately, that takes as long as a week, and in the meantime, Lahana got weaker and weaker. Her stomach was swollen and her liver inflamed, and so Jobson decided she needed surgery. The surgery, which was performed on November 15, revealed that she had been bleeding internally, a sign of viral hemorrhagic fever, but in the absence of confirmation from the lab, they still thought she might have something else, such as typhoid.

Then, later that same day, the laboratory reported that there was a 50 percent chance, based on the viral culture, that Lahana had Ebola. By midnight that had increased to 80 percent, and the next day the lab was certain. Further research revealed that Lahana had contracted the disease while assisting in an operation on a doctor from Gabon, which was suffering an Ebola outbreak at the time. The doctor recovered, and no one ever suspected he had had Ebola—until Lahana became ill.[8]

The fact she had Ebola meant the operation carried out on her by Jobson was enormously risky—and the fact that the diagnosis by viral culture took so long meant the surgical team carrying out that operation did not even know the risk they faced.

And despite extensive treatment in a modern hospital, Lahana died.

TESTING WITH PCR

The fastest and most accurate method of diagnosis is the polymerase chain reaction (PCR) test, which looks for genetic material from the virus and creates enough copies of it that it can be detected. However, as noted earlier, it can take three days for the virus load within a patient to reach detectable levels, even via PCR. Still, it's faster than the ELISA test, and

A child in Gabon stands in front of a home where eight family members died of Ebola. Diagnosing the disease accurately and quickly has been challenging, particularly in areas that do not have the proper technology.

unlike PCR, ELISA will also give positive results even after a patient has recovered.[9]

No matter which method is used, Ebola remains tremendously difficult to diagnose quickly and with certainty. Only laboratories with the necessary high level of biosafety can handle the samples, and the materials used in the tests are not commercially available, which further limits the number of labs equipped to do the tests.

Because the symptoms of Ebola mimic other diseases and because of the difficulty of obtaining a laboratory diagnosis, the first step for hospitals is to make sure they have gathered an accurate patient history: If the person with symptoms has had contact with the blood or body fluids of a person sick with Ebola, contact with objects that have been contaminated with the blood or body fluids of a person sick with Ebola, or contact with infected animals, he should be isolated while samples are collected and tested.

Treating Ebola Virus Disease

O ne of the most terrifying things about Ebola is the fact
that there is no standard treatment for it. Doctors
know this, and they risk exposure every day when they
are working with patients, even when taking all the necessary
precautions.

A frightening example occurred in 1979 in southern Sudan,
where Joe McCormick and Roy Baron of the CDC Special
Pathogens Branch had flown to investigate a new outbreak of
Ebola in the town of Nzara. They collected blood samples from
patients suffering from the disease. The samples were sent back
to the CDC in Atlanta.

Then, they set up a makeshift laboratory and began routinely testing the blood of patients brought in on carts and
stretchers by their families. As McCormick began drawing
blood from one very ill and frail elderly woman, she jerked.
The needle slipped, and he saw with horror a bright red drop
of blood ooze out of the thumb of his glove. He had stuck himself with the needle—and he knew, more than most people, that
when you get stuck by a potentially contaminated needle in the

midst of a deadly epidemic, the odds for survival are not very good.

After some thought, he decided to wait and see if he developed symptoms rather than leave, which would have shut down the investigation. He knew that if he had been infected, he would begin to experience the early symptoms of severe headache, fever, and body pains within three to ten days.

The two CDC doctors had brought with them several units of plasma collected three years before from patients who had survived a previous Ebola outbreak in Nzara. McCormick had Baron set up an intravenous line and give him some of the old plasma.

While he waited to see if he would fall ill, McCormick continued his work and kept particularly close watch on the old woman from whom he had been drawing blood when the accident occurred. One evening he was surprised to see her sitting up and talking to relatives, her fever gone. He knew that if she had recovered from Ebola, as about half those who contract the Sudan virus do, her blood would carry antibodies. If she had those antibodies, it would prove that she had, indeed, had Ebola—and that he had been exposed to it. He ran the necessary tests. Her blood was free of antibodies. He had never been exposed.[1]

But both his fear at the prospect and the fatalism with which he greeted it highlight that one grim inescapable fact: To date, there is no standard treatment for Ebola.

SUPPORTIVE THERAPY

As with other diseases for which there is no standard treatment, patients who are suffering from Ebola receive supportive therapy. This is therapy designed to keep their bodies functioning in the hope that their immune systems will rally to fight off the infection on their own.

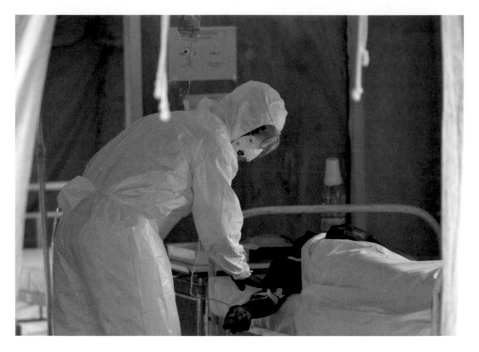

Doctors treating Ebola patients understand they are risking exposure to the disease, even when all proper precautions are taken.

Supportive therapy consists of balancing the patients' fluids and electrolytes, making sure they are getting enough oxygen, trying to keep up their blood pressure, and treating them for any complicating, secondary infections.[2] This maximizes the chances of patients recovering on their own. Unfortunately, this kind of therapy requires a modern hospital, and most Ebola outbreaks occur where medical facilities are primitive. As a result, most of the focus is on stopping the chain of transmission rather than treating patients who already have the disease.

Supportive therapy consists of balancing the patients' fluids and electrolytes, making sure they are getting enough oxygen, trying to keep up their blood pressure, and treating them for any complicating, secondary infections.

For instance, when the outbreak began in Kikwit in 1995, infusions to keep up fluid levels were rarely given to patients, even when they were severely dehydrated, and up to 80 percent of those early patients died. The fatality rate dropped once healthcare workers had been trained in supportive therapy and there were fewer patients overloading the hospitals.[3]

One other treatment was tried in Kikwit, which echoed McCormick's choice to be injected with plasma from survivors of the 1976 outbreak, and it may be the most promising of all in the short term.

During the large outbreak in Kikwit, Zaire, in 1995, eight patients were similarly given blood from patients who had been infected with Ebola but survived. Seven of the eight patients who received the blood also survived. Transfusions were also tried during an outbreak in Gabon in February 1996, where the fatality rate was slightly lower.[4] However, because of the small number of patients involved, it was impossible to say

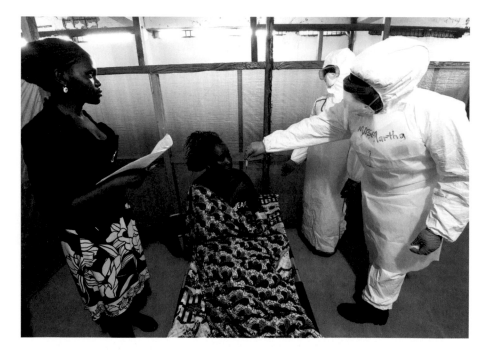

Members of the WHO train new healthcare workers in Liberia. Educating those who care for Ebola patients is an essential step in stopping the disease from spreading.

for certain that the transfusions made the difference. The treatment is also difficult to use because both the donor and recipient must have the same blood type, and there is the risk of transferring other viruses, such as HIV, the virus that causes AIDS.

The massive outbreak of Ebola in West Africa, still ongoing as this book is written, has prompted renewed interest in transfusions as a possible treatment, however. In fact, in September 2014 the WHO announced that treating Ebola patients with blood transfusions from survivors should have top priority among all the experimental therapies under consideration.[5] By the end of 2014, the first studies of blood-based Ebola therapy had begun in Liberia, with studies in Guinea and Sierra Leone starting up early in 2015.[6]

Although there are no proven treatments for Ebola, research is pointing the way toward better treatments in the future, including several drugs and a possible vaccine.

TEARING AT THE SOCIAL FABRIC

O ne of the most tragic aspects of Ebola is the way that it devastates entire families, particularly in countries where access to hospitals and doctors is limited and therefore most people who fall ill are cared for at home. The disease tears apart communities due to a mixture of fear, superstitions, and ignorance. Here is one sad tale that can stand in for many, many similar ones:

In early 1996, a distant relative who lived in the rain forest visited the home of Bernard Massika, chieftain of the village of Epassendje, Gabon. Shortly after that, one by one, Massika's family began to die. The younger of his two wives lapsed into a feverish coma, and her skin turned a deathly blue-black. His eight-year-old daughter began vomiting and coughing up blood. Within a month, ten members of Massika's family— including all nine of his children—had died.

Villagers believed Massika's family was cursed, and so Massika was replaced as chieftain by his younger brother, whose household was not affected. Massika and other relatives were forced to flee from Epassendje. They ended up in the town of Makokou. Massika's remaining wife, Pauline, who had nearly died of the disease, no longer spoke to her family and refused to shake hands with strangers.

Massika was told that the cause of his family's death was something called Ebola, but he did not believe it. "This was not a disease," he said. "We were attacked by powerful spirits of darkness." Other Gabonese felt the same way, blaming Ebola's nasty symptoms on witches, ghouls, and vampires.[1]

The same supernatural explanations surfaced in the outbreak in Uganda in 2000. Justin Okot, a neighbor of Esther Owete, one of the first to die in that outbreak, said, "We did not understand that someone could die that quickly. We began calling this thing '*gemo*,' which in Luo (the local language) is a type of ghost or evil spirit. No one knows about it, but it comes and takes you in the night."[2]

It was the only explanation that made sense to them. The speed with which people died and the horrible way in which they died was too terrifying to put down to mere disease. Surely, they must be victims of black magic. As Massika wondered, "How can I believe all of this was just an accident? My enemies are working against me."[3]

Those who do not believe in black magic may put the disease down to punishment from God. Serafin Emputu, who lived in Kikwit near a house where seven people died, said they died because they did not pray. "I know that the persons who believed firmly in God, believed in Jesus Christ, would not be infected, and my neighbors, they did not pray at all," she said.[4]

DEATH AND DISRUPTION

An outbreak of Ebola has a way of terrifying and disrupting society far out of proportion to the actual number of deaths the disease causes, due to the ways in which it is typically spread: through unsafe practices in hospitals, and through close

Villagers in Meliandou, Guinea, watch as traditional healers perform an exorcism. Many in the village believed the Ebola outbreak was caused by a curse.

contact with family members who have already contracted the disease.

Because the disease has often spread through, and been spread by, hospitals, one of the effects of an outbreak is distrust in doctors and hospitals. This has far-ranging consequences, as people may be less likely to go to the hospital in the future for treatment for diseases that can be cured or controlled.

Because the disease has often spread through, and been spread by, hospitals, one of the effects of an outbreak is distrust in doctors and hospitals.

Ali Kahn, epidemiology chief of the Special Pathogens Branch of the CDC at the time of the 1995 Kikwit outbreak, recalled all sorts of resistance to going to the hospital. "There was a guy who was found hiding in a barrel at his second wife's house, people hiding other cases. For a lot of people, the outbreak was associated with the hospital, and the hospital was where you went to die."[5]

In the months following the end of the Kikwit outbreak, Kikwit General Hospital was almost empty. Before the epidemic, it was often so full that in many wards two people shared every bed. Madar Minioko, a lay pastor in Kikwit, claimed it was because health workers were no longer helping the sick. He said that he went to the hospital with a sick friend who had a high fever from malaria, but the nurse refused to take his blood or give him an injection, instead asking the friend's wife to do it. Minioko said it was not an unusual story, and it made him so mad he would rather die at home than go to a clinic or hospital.[6]

The workers at the hospital denied anyone was being refused treatment, but admitted they were afraid. "Before the epidemic, even when we did not have the protective material, we worked, and we were touching patients, and we had

The family of Dr. Matthew Lukwiya gather around his portrait. Dr. Lukwiya died treating Ebola patients in a dangerous area of Uganda where many doctors refused to work.

confidence and trust in our patients," said a chief surgical nurse. "But, since this epidemic, we have seen many of our colleagues have died. That is why we are afraid."[7]

That fear is justified, since so many healthcare workers have died in the various Ebola outbreaks. And the loss of nurses and doctors is another blow the disease deals to the communities in which it surfaces. One of the victims of the Ugandan outbreak in 2000, for instance, was Dr. Matthew Lukwiya, the medical superintendent of Lacor Hospital in Gulu. Summoned back to Gulu from Kampala when patients began dying, he was the one who recognized that the mysterious disease might be Ebola and, after confirmation from South African laboratories, raised the global alarm.

By using modern nursing techniques and educating the local population about how the disease was spread, he managed to contain the outbreak to the immediate region. It is safe to say that without his early efforts, the outbreak would have been much worse. Unfortunately, at some point he must have failed to take the proper precautions himself. He fell ill on November 30 and died on December 5.[8] "Ebola virus is not very forgiving," said Dr. Ray Arthur, the WHO Ebola coordinator in Gulu. "One little mistake is enough to infect an individual."[9] Lukwiya was the fourteenth medical worker to die in the Ugandan outbreak.

In the current West African epidemic, the toll has been far higher: As of the beginning of 2015, more than eight hundred healthcare workers had been infected and almost five hundred had died.[10]

The health systems in the hardest-hit countries of Guinea, Liberia, and Sierra Leone lacked sufficient amounts of drugs, ambulances, facilities, trained health personnel, and many other items needed to control the outbreak. Again, the shortage of protective equipment resulted in multiple infections and deaths among medical personnel, further spreading the disease

A nine-year-old girl cries outside her home in Monrovia, Liberia, after learning that her mother, who was taken away to an Ebola ward the day before, has died.

and leading people to avoid treatment for fear of being infected. Making things worse was the fact that poor rural areas have much more limited access to health services than urban areas: Conakry, which is home to just 15 percent of the population of Guinea, has 75 percent of the health workers, whereas the Guinée forest district, which has been hardest hit, is home to 22 percent of the Guinean population, but has only nine percent of the health workers.[11]

A BLOW TO TRADITIONS

Traditional lifestyles are another victim of Ebola. In the cultures in which it has surfaced, family members care for people who are sick, and when someone dies, family members prepare the body for burial. Unfortunately, because Ebola is transmitted by contact with bodily fluids, both of these are high-risk activities. So are other seemingly ordinary activities such as embracing friends and family and sharing eating utensils.

One of the things Dr. Lukwiya did to contain the Ugandan outbreak was to convince radio broadcasters to tell Gulu residents what they could do to protect themselves: avoiding shaking hands, sharing cups or plates, and particularly, taking part in the traditional ritualistic, communal washing of the dead.[12] When Dr. Lukwiya himself was buried, his body was sealed within a plastic shroud; his pallbearers wore latex gloves and surgical masks; and his friends and family were not allowed to touch the body.[13]

The necessity of abandoning traditional funeral practices is particularly hard on communities suffering from so much unexpected, horrible death. As Madar Minioko put it, in Kikwit, "Before, it was our custom to never leave a corpse alone. When someone died, all the family and the clan were always around the body, touching it and crying over it. We washed the body, changed its clothes, arranged it in a comfortable coffin, and only then did we feel we had respected and properly buried the relative."[14]

That stopped during the outbreak. Teams of Red Cross workers dressed in helmets, boots, gloves, and goggles simply gathered the bodies, zipped them into body bags, and buried them without ceremony.

EVEN SURVIVORS SUFFER

Surviving the disease does not necessarily make things any easier. James Akena, a farmer, contracted Ebola and survived during the outbreak in Gulu, Uganda. When he was released from the hospital, he was given a letter certifying that he could "go home and is no longer dangerous to his community."

"When I was discharged a nurse took me home," he said. "We found my house and all my belongings burned, and my neighbors chased us away."[15] With no home and no money, Akena spent several days without food in an outdoor bus station until health workers who were following up on his case discovered him. Eventually, the government resettled him into another part of Uganda.

Lucy Akidi had a similar story. "When my in-laws heard that I was discharged, they sent someone to tell me to go straight to my parents' compound and never return to theirs. But my husband resisted and said I would return, even if it meant living in isolation. My in-laws fled when we arrived."[16]

This pattern has continued in the massive West African outbreak. In Conakry, Guinea, a woman named Jamila survived Ebola, only to get a cold reception when she returned home after twelve days in an isolation ward. She was fired from her job as a philosophy teacher because of fear she would infect her students.

"People looked at me like I'd come back from the dead, like I was a zombie," Jamila said (she wouldn't give reporters her name for fear of being more widely identified as an Ebola

Beatrice Yordolo (in the yellow shirt) is the the last survivor of the Ebola virus in Liberia. Many people who survive the disease must deal with fear and prejudice when they return to their neighborhoods.

survivor.) "Nobody except my relatives wanted anything to do with me anymore."[17]

These kinds of fears are common wherever Ebola surfaces, and make it imperative that medical workers explain as clearly as possible how the disease is transmitted and that survivors are not infectious.

WORLDWIDE PARANOIA

But paranoia is not confined to the places directly affected by Ebola. The whole world, it sometimes seems, is paranoid about Ebola, which makes every outbreak of the disease big news.

The outbreak doesn't even have to be real. In February 2001 Colette Matshimoseka fell ill in Hamilton, Ontario, after arriving on a visit from the Democratic Republic of the Congo. She was admitted to the hospital with a high fever. Doctors did not know what was wrong with her, but because she had come from the Congo, they isolated her and sent samples of her blood to the CDC and Canada's own Level 4 Biosafety Laboratory in Winnipeg, Manitoba. All the major television news networks sent reporters to the hospital, and doctors gave daily news conferences until it was determined that she did not, in fact, have Ebola. Then the news interest vanished.[18]

To put it in perspective, as of this writing, the West African Ebola outbreak has killed about ten thousand people while in 2012 AIDS killed about 1.1 million in sub-Saharan Africa. Lower respiratory-tract infections (such as tuberculosis and pneumonia) killed another 1.1 million. Malaria killed 568,000. Diarrhea—which people joke about in North America—killed 644,000.[19]

So why does Ebola fascinate and frighten people so much?

"It has to do with public perception," says Dr. Jay Keystone, a physician at Toronto General Hospital's Centre for Travel and Tropical Medicine. "Suddenly this is the plague. Ebola is in our face, through the media. That is why we're so afraid of it."[20]

Media crews set up across from the Maine home of Kaci Hickox, a nurse who had recently returned from caring for Ebola patients in Sierra Leone. Journalists and television crews followed her when she challenged her mandatory quarantine. Hickox never tested positive for the virus.

"VILIFIED IN THE MEDIA"

While treating patients with Ebola in Guinea in 2014, Dr. Craig Spencer became infected. He returned to the United States before he had any symptoms, and on October 23, 2014, was admitted to Bellevue Hospital as New York City's first Ebola patient. He later wrote that, even though he was too sick to realize it, "I was being vilified in the media even as my liver was failing and my fiancée was quarantined in our apartment. . . . My activities before I was hospitalized were widely reported and highly criticized. People feared riding the subway or going bowling because of me. The whole country soon knew where I like to walk, eat, and unwind."[21]

Despite the personal attacks, he said he understands the fear that gripped the country, because he had felt it himself. "People fear the unknown, and fear in measured doses can be therapeutic and inform rational responses, but in excess, it fosters poor decision making that can be harmful. After my diagnosis, the media and politicians could have educated the public about Ebola. Instead, they spent hours retracing my steps through New York and debating whether Ebola can be transmitted through a bowling ball. . . . The media sold hype with flashy headlines and fabricated stories about my personal life and the threat I posed to public health, abdicating their responsibility for informing public opinion and influencing public policy."[22]

He added, "I know how real the fear of Ebola is, but we need to overcome it. We all lose when we allow irrational fear, fueled in part by prime-time ratings and political expediency, to supersede pragmatic public health preparedness."[23]

A BESTSELLING BOOK STARTS THE HYPE

Public perception of Ebola as a particularly frightening disease probably began with a story by Richard Preston called "Crisis in the Hot Zone," which was published in *The New Yorker* on October 26, 1992. That eventually became the book *The Hot Zone*. That book in turn inspired *Outbreak*, a movie starring Dustin Hoffman, in which a fictional Ebola-like disease threatens the United States. Then there was a TV movie, *Virus*, starring Ebola itself. *The Coming Plague*, a Pulitzer Prize-winning book by Laurie Garrett, also suggests that an apocalyptic outbreak of Ebola or some other, currently unknown, disease could be just around the corner. Newspapers and magazines have also frequently contributed sensationalized articles and stories.

The fear of Ebola is based on certain common misconceptions about Ebola, including that it is highly contagious, that it is the deadliest disease known to man, and that it could cause an epidemic in North America.

In fact, according to the CDC, the risk of an outbreak in the United States is very low because Ebola is not spread through casual contact. "We know how to stop Ebola's further spread: thorough case finding, isolation of ill people, contacting people exposed to the ill person, and further isolation of contacts if they develop symptoms."[24]

Although there have been cases of Ebola in the United States linked to the current West African epidemic, there has as yet been no outbreak of the disease.

EBOLA MYTHS

Here are five myths about Ebola that many people believe:

1. Ebola is highly contagious. *Actually, compared to most common diseases, it isn't. The primary risk is coming in contact with the bodily fluids of people who are visibly infected: blood, saliva, vomit, and possibly sweat. The virus can then be transferred to the mucous membrane. In the West African epidemic, each patient has infected on average two healthy people. By way of comparison, each patient in the 2002–2003 SARS outbreak infected five people; someone with mumps will, on average, infect ten people; and people with measles will infect a whopping eighteen.*[25]

2. You can catch Ebola from someone who looks perfectly healthy. *This fear is one reason people have been uneasy about anyone who has recently returned from West Africa. In fact, generally speaking people who aren't yet displaying symptoms aren't infectious.*[26]

3. If you catch Ebola, you'll almost certainly die. *While in past outbreaks the death rate for those infected with Ebola has been up to 90 percent, in the current epidemic the rate is 74 percent. That's still high, but it also reflects the poor state of health care in the affected regions. There have so far been nine Ebola patients in the United States: Of those, eight have survived, a fatality rate of only 10 percent.*[27]

4. We should quarantine anyone with Ebola-like symptoms. *This is impractical, because "Ebola-like" symptoms are also "flu-like" symptoms, and flu-like symptoms are common.*

5. Ebola is the biggest public health disaster imaginable. *In fact, Ebola, though a local public health disaster and a concern worldwide, is nowhere near the top of the list of things epidemiologists worry about: number one is a deadly flu pandemic. The Spanish flu outbreak of 1918 killed millions worldwide, and unlike the influenza that strikes every year, killed young, healthy people. So far we've avoided a repeat, but there's no guarantee we'll be that lucky forever.*[28]

6. The virus could rapidly mutate into a form that could be transmitted through the air. *As noted earlier, although all viruses mutate, Ebola is an unlikely candidate to mutate into an airborne version. It is an ancient, relatively stable virus, and would require multiple mutations to become transmissible via air.*[29]

The fact is, if you live in a developed western country, the chances of Ebola affecting you personally are exceedingly small.

Chapter 7

PREVENTATIVE MEASURES

W hen you're dealing with a disease like Ebola that has no standard treatment, preventing the spread of the disease once it appears becomes paramount. Over the decades doctors have learned what needs to be done to break the chain of transmission. Most outbreaks have been fairly quickly contained. But not, unfortunately, the most recent one in West Africa.

In 1976 when Ebola surfaced for the first time in Yambuku, one of the nuns who was infected, Sister M. E., flew to Kinshasa with another nun, Sister E.R., and a priest. All three were admitted to Ngaliema Hospital, where they were attended by Margaretha Isaäcson, a South African physician, and a Zairian nurse named Mayinga.

Later, Isaäcson explained how she dealt with her three new patients. "From the moment of the arrival of the two nuns and the priest . . . some precautionary measures were taken to prevent spread of the infection," she said. "Barrier nursing was introduced at the start, and cotton gowns and cotton masks were worn when attending the patient. These were later

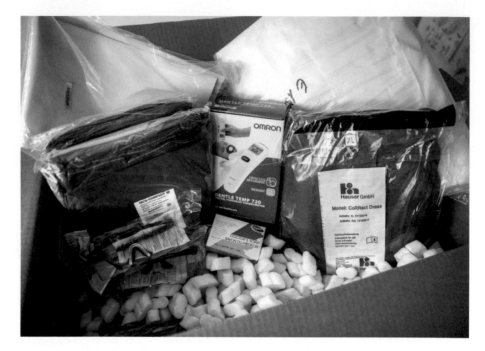

Many charities donated health kits like this one during the 2014 Ebola outbreak. The kits contain basic safety items like protective clothing, gloves, masks, soap, and water purification pills.

replaced by disposable gowns and masks, but as supplies were inadequate, the gowns and the disposable plastic overshoes were hung up outside the door of the patient's room for reuse." Isaäcson also noted that Sister E. R. did not wear protective clothing when attending Sister M. E.[1]

Sister M. E. died on September 30. Eight days later, Sister E. R. fell ill; she died on October 14. In the entire hospital, one of the biggest in the city, the only other person who acquired the disease was nurse Mayinga, who had been in contact with the first nun for several days prior to her death. Researchers assume that at some point she failed to follow proper safety procedures.

Nobody else got the disease, even though Mayinga, after she developed symptoms, spent several hours in a crowded emergency room at Mama Yemo Hospital (also in Kinshasa), where she shared a bottle of soda with a young boy and shared food off the plate of a fourteen-year-old girl.

BARRIER NURSING

Isaäcson concluded that "it appears that the observation of the basic principles of aseptic technique or barrier nursing are probably effective in breaking the chain of infection," that "air-borne dissemination of the virus did not play a major role, if any, in the transmission of the disease," and "the Ebola virus is not highly infectious and requires very close contact, primarily with blood or secretions, for its transmission."[2]

More than three decades later, those conclusions remain intact. The spread of Ebola, once an outbreak has occurred, can be halted with fairly simple safety precautions that basically consist of isolating people who are infected and erecting a barrier around them, and by ensuring those who tend to them wear protective clothing.

STEP-BY-STEP PROCEDURES

The World Health Organization provides precise guidelines for dealing with patients with suspected Ebola virus disease. To begin with, noting that it's not always easy to identify those with Ebola because its initial symptoms are similar to those of other diseases, the WHO says it is important that healthcare workers apply certain standard precautions with all patients, regardless of their diagnosis. These precautions include good hand hygiene; using disposable medical examination gloves before contact with body fluids, mucous membranes, broken skin and contaminated items; and wearing gowns and eye protection during any procedures that might result in contact with body fluids.

Since one of the greatest dangers for healthcare workers is accidental contamination via cuts and punctures, special care should be taken to safely handle and dispose of sharp instruments, and to thoroughly clean and disinfect all reusable equipment. Suspected Ebola patients should be isolated in single rooms if possible, or at least in specific confined areas, with restricted access. Staff and equipment should be exclusively assigned to those areas, and not allowed to interact with other patients.

Even cleaners should wear rubber gloves, an impermeable gown and boots, and facial protection if there's a risk of splashes or contact with blood and body fluids—that includes when handling bed linen. Surfaces and contaminated objects should be cleaned and then disinfected as soon as possible (one standard, and effective, disinfectant is a 0.5% chlorine solution). Soiled linen should be placed in clearly labeled, leak-proof bags or buckets at the site of use and the container surfaces should be disinfected before the containers are taken to the laundry area, where the linen should be washed with water and detergent, and, if laundered at low-temperature, soaked in 0.05% chlorine for approximately thirty minutes before being dried.

PERSONAL PROTECTIVE EQUIPMENT

According to the World Health Organization, standard personal protective equipment (PPE) that should be worn when working with Ebola patients includes:

• Correctly sized non-sterile exam gloves or surgical gloves;
• A disposable, long-sleeve, impermeable gown to cover clothing and exposed skin;
• A medical mask and eye protection (goggles or face shield); Closed, puncture- and fluid-resistant shoes (e.g. rubber boots).
Additional PPE, depending on what tasks are being carried out, may include:
• A waterproof apron, if the gown is not impermeable;
• Disposable overshoes and leg coverings, if boots are not available;
• Heavy duty (rubber) gloves, when performing environmental cleaning or handling waste;
• A respirator capable of filtering out the virus, if the procedure might result in a spray of airborne particles.[3]

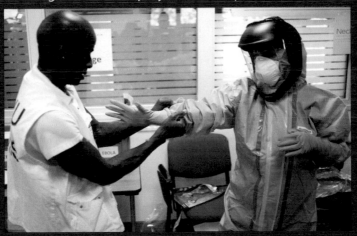

A healthcare worker is helped into her protective gear during a training exercise. Safety precautions like these are the first line of defense against the spread of Ebola.

Tests should be limited to those absolutely essential for diagnosis and care, and anyone collecting or handling specimens should wear full PPE, including respirators. All laboratory sample processing should take place under a safety cabinet with exhaust ventilation.

When patients die, autopsies should be limited and only performed by trained personnel wearing full PPE, including double gloves and disposable impermeable gowns. Any samples or fluids being disposed of should be incinerated. The handling of human remains should be kept to a minimum, and again only by those wearing proper PPE. The body shouldn't be sprayed, washed, or embalmed. It should be placed in a double bag, which is then wiped over with a disinfectant, and labeled as containing highly infectious material. The body should then be immediately moved to the mortuary, placed inside a coffin if possible, and buried promptly.

Anyone working with a known or suspected Ebola patient who is exposed, through mucous membranes or a break in the skin, to the bodily fluids from the patient should leave the patient care area, wash his or her affected skin surfaces with soap and water, and irrigate mucous membranes (such as the lining of the eye) with lots and lots of water or eyewash solution. Follow-up care consists of monitoring fever twice daily for twenty-one days after the incident.[4]

In other words, if you've been exposed, all you can do is wait.

PREVENTING OUTBREAKS DIFFICULT

Preventing the spread of Ebola in a healthcare setting, then, is not that difficult. Plastic and rubber stop it cold, and ordinary bleach kills it. But preventing the spread of the disease is not the same as preventing the disease. To do that, you need to either create a vaccine or discover where the disease is hiding in the wild. As you'll read in the next chapter, there are

Sanitary treatment of the dead infected with Ebola is an important part of containing the disease.

promising signs a vaccine could be on the horizon—but we don't have one yet.

As for finding the disease in the wild, we're not there yet, at least not definitively. But we're close. We know that Ebola has to lurk in an animal species somewhere, because the virus kills humans too quickly for humans to be a good host. Viruses reproduce by taking over the genetic machinery of a living host cell. They can't live on their own; when a virus's host dies, it dies, too. That means Ebola must be living peaceably inside some other living creature, only occasionally making the jump to humans or monkeys.

After each outbreak, scientists have scoured the surrounding countryside, collecting samples of all kinds of plants and animals, looking for one that contains Ebola. Hundreds of species of animals and plants have been examined. The only way to prove that a particular animal is carrying Ebola is to culture live virus from its tissues or blood, and so far, that hasn't been achieved. So we still can't say for certain what the animal reservoir species is. But increasingly, circumstantial evidence is pointing to bats.

Ebola must be living peaceably inside some other living creature, only occasionally making the jump to humans or monkeys.

During the 2007 outbreak in the Democratic Republic of Congo, which affected more than 260 people and killed 186, a research team interviewed villagers who reported that, although there had been no unusual illness among wild or domestic animals in the region, there had been a massive annual fruit bat migration, with migrating bats settling in the outbreak area for several weeks, between April and May. The villagers killed many of them for food. The researchers were able to show that the person identified as the first victim had bought freshly killed bats from hunters to eat just before falling ill.[5]

A study published late in 2014 suggests that the reason the 2014 Ebola epidemic began with a single sick child, as described earlier, was because young Emile Oumouno contracted the disease from a small insect-eating bat—so small that only children hunt it, not adults (who do hunt the larger, meatier species of bats).[6]

Within weeks of news of the outbreak, a team led by Fabian Leendertz of the Robert Koch Institute in Berlin, consisting of ecologists and veterinarians and an anthropologist to interview local people, traveled to Guinea. When they studied the wildlife in the forests there, they saw no sign of a die-off in the larger animals, such as monkeys and chimpanzees, who are also susceptible to Ebola, which suggested that this time (unlike some previous outbreaks, which were linked to people handling the meat of infected chimpanzees or monkeys) the virus had jumped directly from the reservoir species to humans.

The team traveled to Meliandou, where Emile had contracted the disease in December 2013. His mother, sister, and grandmother soon died, but no adult males dies in that initial wave of illness from the outbreak, which seemed to indicate it had not come from bushmeat.

After interviewing survivors and collecting samples, including blood and tissue from captured bats, the team began to suspect that the reservoir host was a bat, but a very particular kind of bat not previously considered: small, insect-eating bats, locally called "lolibelo," which roost in natural recesses like hollow trees—and under the roofs of houses. Children hunt and kill the bats, which are about the size of mice, roasting them over fires like hot dogs. A large flock of the bats had been roosting in a hollow tree. Although the tree had been recently burned, Leendertz's was able to recover DNA from the soil at the tree's base to identify the bat as *Mops condylurus*, the

Angolan free-tailed bat. The hollow tree had apparently been a favorite play spot for the small children of the village, including little Emile.

It's still just circumstantial evidence. Although Angolan free-tailed bats have been found to contain antibodies against Ebola virus, that was from a very small sample. Until now, the species hasn't been considered a prime candidate. Leendertz and his colleagues have conducted extensive further sampling in Ivory Coast, also caught up in the current outbreak. As of this writing, the jury is still out on whether the reservoir species— or, more likely, *one* reservoir species—of Ebola virus has been found.[7]

A man in Uganda holds a bat that has been captured for food. Researchers have long suspected the fruit bat of carrying the Ebola virus but now are looking at the possibility that a different kind of bat is responsible for the 2014 West Africa outbreak.

Chapter 8

LOOKING TO THE FUTURE

W hen Ebola first appeared in 1976, it was terrifying partly because it was a completely unknown disease; no one knew anything about it at all. Twenty years later, at the time of the 1995 Ebola outbreak in Kiwit, things hadn't improved much. Even as the new outbreak took hold a group of researchers were working on a paper entitled "Filoviridae: Marburg and Ebola Viruses," intended to summarize everything that was then known about these two hemorrhagic fever viruses. The paper was published in 1996. Rather than summarizing knowledge, however, it mostly summarized lack of knowledge.

"We still do not know how filoviruses are maintained in nature," the authors wrote. "The mode of entry of Marburg and Ebola viruses into cells remains unknown," they also stated. The means by which the viruses caused such devastating symptoms still were not understood. The authors noted that in fatal infections, patients died with high levels of virus particles in their systems but no sign of an immune response, for reasons unknown. They pointed out that no one knew how or why some people recovered and some did not. "The origin in nature and the natural history of Marburg and Ebola viruses remain a mystery," they wrote.[1]

But in the years since, we have found the beginnings of answers to some of these mysteries, in the process creating hope that in the not-too-distant future, we may have drugs that can treat Ebola effectively—or even a vaccine that can protect people from contracting it in the first place.

THE GENETIC KEY

Despite the general state of ignorance about the virus in 1996, at least one vital piece of information had been uncovered by the time the paper was written: the Ebola virus's precise genetic makeup.

Genes are the basic unit of heredity; they contain the information passed on from generation to generation of an organism. The Ebola virus has seven genes. Each gene, in turn, is made up of many thousands of pairs of "bases," the chemicals that serve as a kind of language in which the information for making new copies of the organism is written. Anthony Sanchez of the CDC decoded and published the precise combination of molecular bases that made up six of Ebola's seven genes; a group of Russian scientists decoded the seventh.

The complete list of bases contained in all the genes in an organism is called the genome. The Ebola genome turned out to be very large for a virus, meaning that more information is contained in an Ebola virus than in many other viruses.

To determine what a particular gene does in an organism, you can separate it from the rest of the organism's genes and insert it into a cell culture. Since genes tell cells what substances to synthesize, you can sometimes tell what a particular gene does by figuring out what the cells inoculated with the separated gene are synthesizing that they would not normally.

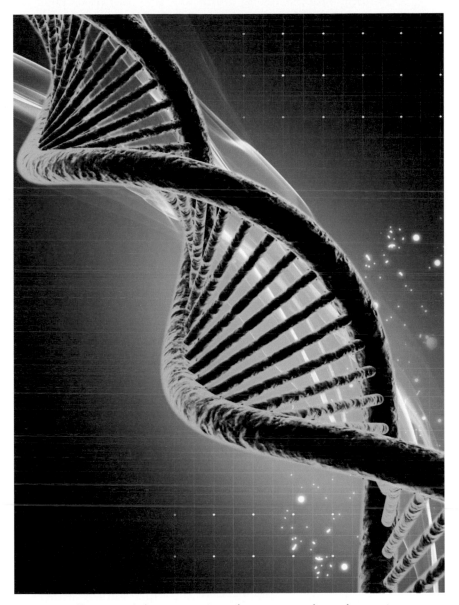

DNA, illustrated here, carries the genes that determine an organism's characteristics. Scientists have been trying to use their knowledge of Ebola's genetic makeup to find treatments for the virus.

One thing Sanchez found out in his study of Ebola's genes was that one gene did something "very bizarre." Whereas normally one gene results in only one output from a cell, one of Ebola's genes resulted in the creation of two substances: One was the outer surface of the virus, a spiky coat that attaches to molecules on the surfaces of cells and allows the virus to gain entry to it. The other substance, however, was a liquid that did not become part of the virus at all, but instead simply floated away.[2]

No one was sure what purpose that substance, called a glycoprotein, served; however, a comparison of the gene that produces the glycoprotein with other viral genetic codes in a database revealed that one small region of the glycoprotein gene was very similar to sections of one of the genes of cancer-causing retroviruses that had been shown to work to weaken the action of the body's immune system. That raised the possibility that Ebola's glycoprotein gene helped explain why Ebola victims seemed to mount no effective immune system response to infection with the virus.[3]

Then, in July 2000, Dr. Gary Nabel of the NIH Vaccine Research Center and his team from the NIH and the CDC said they had discovered that the glycoprotein attacks the cells that line blood vessels, called endothelial cells, making them leak and possibly causing much of the devastating hemorrhaging characteristic of the disease.

Nabel's team genetically engineered cultured human endothelial cells so that they produced the Ebola glycoprotein, and found that within twenty-four hours, the cells could no longer stick to one another. The cells all died within a few days.

When the gene coding for glycoprotein was introduced directly into blood vessels surgically removed from pigs or humans, the vessels suffered massive losses of endothelial cells within two days. They became leaky, letting fluids through much more easily.[4] Nabel's team also discovered that the Ebola-

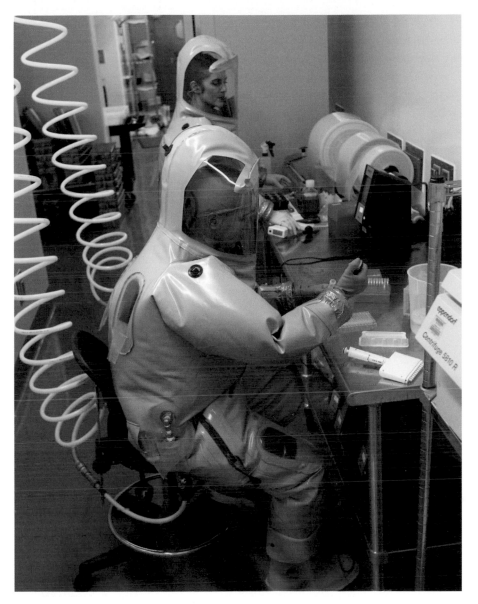

Scientists conduct Ebola research at a Biosafety Level 4 lab in 2014.

Reston version of Ebola does not damage blood vessels in the same way, which could explain why it is not fatal to humans.

By testing how live Ebola virus attacks different cells in the laboratory, and observing the disease's progression in nonhuman primates, researchers have learned more about the disease's mechanism over the past decade and a half. They have found that Ebola both targets the immune system and damages blood vessels, two tricks that are central to its devastating impact on the body.

HOW EBOLA KILLS

When Ebola enters the body, it infects dendritic cells—cells that normally display signs of infection on their surface to activate white blood cells, known as T lymphocytes. These T cells work to destroy infected cells before the virus they contain can replicate. Since that "We're infected!" signal is never issued by the dendritic cells, the T cells don't do anything; and when the T cells don't take action, no antibodies, another line of immune-system defense, are activated. That allows the virus to replicate quickly.[5]

Another anti-immune-system trick of the virus was discovered in October 2000, when the outbreak in Uganda was in full swing. A team of German and American researchers published a paper announcing that they had found a protein, called VP35, which Ebola uses to disable the production of interferon. Interferon is a compound produced by the immune system to kill virus-infected cells before they can spew more viruses into the system. Those who fight off Ebola successfully may have a stronger immune system that is able to fight off the effects of this protein, the researchers said. They noted that at least one case had been reported of a person who was infected with Ebola but never developed symptoms.[6]

T cells are not infected by the virus, just prevented from acting. Other white blood cells, called macrophages, *are*

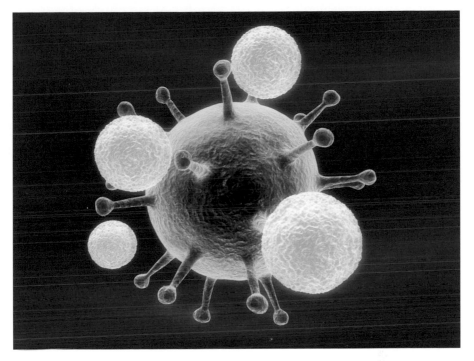

An illustration shows a T cell attacking a virus. These "killer" T cells are a key part of our body's immune system. With the Ebola virus, T cells lose their ability to fight disease.

infected by the virus after they eat it up in the course of performing their normal function of removing cellular debris and foreign material from the bloodstream. The macrophages release proteins that cause blood to clot. These small clots throughout the blood vessels reduce blood supply to organs. The infected macrophages also produce other proteins that trigger inflammation, along with nitric oxide, which damages the lining of blood vessels, causing them to leak.

The system-wide inflammation and fever makes the patient very sick and can damage organs, and Ebola also directly damages many types of tissues by infecting the cells and destroying them from the inside. The disease is particularly destructive to the liver, where Ebola kills cells that produce coagulation proteins and other important components of plasma.

In the gastrointestinal tract, the damage to cells leads to diarrhea, which puts patients at risk of dehydration. In the adrenal gland, Ebola destroys the cells that make steroids, which regulate blood pressure. This leads to circulatory failure, which can starve organs of oxygen, damaging them further.

What ultimately kills Ebola patients? Multiple organ failure, as the virus attacks tissues throughout the body, and shock, due to the drop in blood pressure caused by damage to blood vessels. Some people survive with good supportive therapy, as mentioned earlier in the book, which gives their body time to fight off the infection. There also seems to be a genetic factor: Researchers studying blood samples from patients during the Uganda outbreak in 2000 found genetic markers that predicted who was more likely to survive. The ones who recovered had higher levels of activated T cells, and also certain variants of a gene that codes for the surface proteins white blood cells use to communicate. In 2014 researchers also found that patients with higher levels of a protein called sCD40L, produced by platelets, had a better chance of survival, possibly because it helped the body repair damaged blood vessels.[7]

There are still a lot of questions about how Ebola works in the body. The more that is known, the more targets researchers have for drugs that might treat the disease.

POSSIBLE TREATMENTS

There are a lot of drugs currently being examined as possible Ebola treatments. The WHO tracks drugs in four categories: drugs already in clinical trials in West Africa (only one so far); drugs prioritized for human trials but for which trials are not yet underway (six); drugs that have been given to a few patients more or less in the hope they might do some good, but that have not been formally tested; and drugs that have shown promising anti-Ebola activity in the laboratory but need further research before human trials can proceed.

The only drug currently undergoing clinical testing as this book was being written was Favipiravir, discovered in Japan. It's an antiviral drug that acts against many RNA viruses, not just Ebola, by inhibiting their reproduction. It has already been approved in Japan for treating influenza. A clinical trial began in Guinea in December 2014, but preliminary results issued in February were inconclusive, so tests are continuing as of this writing.[8] Several other drugs are either undergoing safety testing or could be heading to efficacy testing soon. All have shown promising results in the lab, but the jury is still out on whether any of them will be effective Ebola treatments.

EXCITING VACCINE DEVELOPMENTS

While drugs to treat Ebola are important, the best way to stop outbreaks from ever reaching epidemic proportions again would be the development of a vaccine—and it looks like we could be getting close.

Efforts to find a vaccine for Ebola go back many years. In 1997 Dr. Gary Nabel and colleagues reported that guinea pigs injected with genes from the Ebola virus gained protection

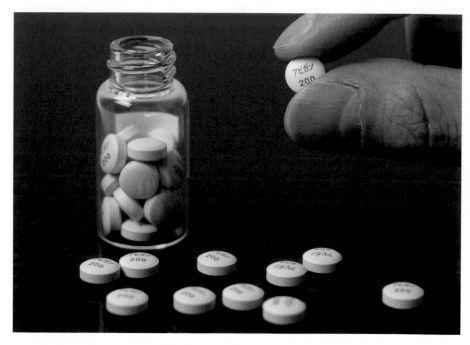

Favipiravir is an antiviral drug that is in clinical testing to treat Ebola. It is currently used to treat influenza.

against infection from it. In those tests, one group of guinea pigs was vaccinated, then injected with Ebola virus within two months. Fifteen of sixteen vaccinated guinea pigs survived. Six animals that had not been vaccinated were also injected with Ebola; all died.[9]

Three years later, Nabel and colleagues reported that four vaccinated macaque monkeys survived an injection of Ebola-Zaire, while unvaccinated control animals died within four to seven days. The vaccine also protected them against Ebola-Taï Forest and Ebola-Sudan, the other two strains of Ebola that cause disease in humans.[10] But no actual vaccine came out of either of those efforts. Outbreaks were relatively small and usually fairly easily contained—until the epidemic in West Africa. Suddenly there are several vaccines in development, and the efforts to have them tested and approved have been fast-tracked so that they are being developed much more quickly than is typical of new treatments.

In early 2015, the first phase of a project called Partnership for Research on Ebola Vaccines in Liberia (PREVAIL), sponsored by the National Institute of Allergy and Infectious Disease (NAID), showed that two experimental Ebola vaccines appeared to be safe, based on the valuation of more than six hundred people in Liberia who took part in the safety study.

Suddenly there are several vaccines in development, and the efforts to have them tested and approved have been fast-tracked so that they are being developed much more quickly than is typical of new treatments.

The PREVAIL trial, which began in Monrovia, Liberia, was designed to test the safety and efficacy of two candidate vaccines: cAd3-EBOZ, co-developed by NAID scientists and the drug company GlaxoSmithKline, and VSV-ZEBOV, developed by the Public Health Agency of Canada and licensed to NewLink Genetics Corporation and Merck.[11] The two vaccines take different approaches. In the VSV-ZEBOV vaccine, a protein from the Zaire strain of Ebola—the one causing the epidemic—is spliced into VSV, a virus that infects cows, horses, pigs, and insects. Part of the VSV virus is extracted and the Ebola protein inserted in its place. VSV is relatively harmless to humans but can replicate in the human body, triggering an immune response not only to VSV but also to the Ebola protein.

On the other hand, cAd3-EBOZ uses a chimpanzee-derived cold virus to deliver genetic material from the Ebola virus. However, unlike VSV-ZEBOV vaccine, it's non-replicating, which could mean larger or repeated doses will be needed to ensure immunity.[12]

In the first phase, volunteers are assigned at random to receive a single injection of either cAd3-EBOZ, VSV-ZEBOV, or a harmless saline solution, or placebo. The trial is what's called "double-blind": Neither the volunteer subjects nor the staff know which injection they are receiving.

Although the initial results proved the vaccines safe, the researchers were continuing to enroll subjects through April 2015 to boost the number of subjects to around 1,500, partly to increase the percentage of women from the initial 16 percent. Subjects will continue to be followed for at least a year, with additional blood samples six and twelve months after vaccination to see how durable the observed immune responses are.

For the final phase of the PREVAIL trial, designed to test the efficacy of the vaccines, investigators had planned to enroll 27,000 people in Liberia at risk of Ebola infection—but as April began, there had been only one new confirmed case of Ebola infection in the country since February 19. Because of that, the scientists leading the trial decided it would be scientifically appropriate to expand the trial to additional sites in other West

African countries, although details hadn't been announced as this book was being written.[13]

One of the most remarkable things about the vaccine trials has been the speed at which they've taken place. Professor Sanjeev Krishna of the Institute for Infection and Immunity at St. George's Hospital in London watched as the research was pushed through after an initial WHO meeting that began on September 3, 2014. The whole process began from scratch at that meeting. "Before then, it was just a blank sheet of paper, and we had to do everything within a few months," he said. The group designed the initial small-scale safety studies, whose

A volunteer from Guinea is administered the VSV-ZEBOV vaccine during clinical trials in 2015. He will be monitored over the next year to see how his immune system responds.

preliminary results, which showed that the side effects, typically fever and joint soreness, were short-lived and not serious, led to the larger PREVAIL study in Liberia mentioned above.

"It was extremely challenging, but also very, very, exciting to think we had the chance to work on something that could be turned around very quickly and might make a difference," Krishna said.

Although the effectiveness of the two vaccines currently being tested, and others being developed, is still to be determined, the lessons learned in fast-tracking these vaccines will be valuable not only the next time there is an Ebola outbreak, but the next time any new disease strikes, whether its something as novel as Ebola, or an influenza pandemic.

"We're going to have to change things," Krishna told *Wired. co.uk*. "Things were so slow to start with, and there wasn't a proper response system setup globally to deal with this kind of issue. Now there are all sorts of people looking at this at different levels, and it has to be looked at urgently. We have to have a system that will readily be able to cope not just with Ebola, but SARS or a flu pandemic. We've just got to do better."[14]

Despite the horror of the West African epidemic, one thing seems clear: The next time Ebola raises its ugly head, the world will be better prepared for it. And maybe, just maybe, vaccines and treatments now in development will nip the epidemic in the bud—and lessen the toll that this devastating plague takes on these impoverished countries. We may not be able to stamp out Ebola completely. But we may get to the point where it is no longer the world's most feared disease.

Top 10 Questions
and Answers

What is Ebola?

Ebola virus disease is a severe, often fatal, disease that affects humans and nonhuman primates (monkeys and chimpanzees). It is caused by infection with a virus of the family *Filoviridae,* genus *Ebolavirus.* It was named after a river in the Democratic Republic of the Congo in Africa, near the place where Ebola first surfaced in 1976.

Is there more than one kind of Ebola?

Yes. In fact, there are five different strains that we know of: Zaire, Sudan, Taï Forest, Bundibugyo, and Reston. The first four have all caused disease in humans. The Reston virus has caused disease in nonhuman primates, but not in humans.

Where is Ebola found in nature?

We do not know for certain. However, researchers believe the most likely animal host is fruit bats, from which it makes the jump to humans, monkeys, and chimpanzees.

Where do outbreaks of Ebola Virus Disease occur?

Confirmed outbreaks of Ebola have been reported in the Democratic Republic of the Congo, Gabon, Sudan, the Ivory Coast, Uganda, and Guinea. In the 2014 West African epidemic, which began in Guinea, the disease spread into Sierra Leone and Liberia. Additional cases were reported in Nigeria, Senegal, Spain, Mali, the United Kingdom, and the United States. Ebola-Reston has caused illness and death in monkeys imported into American research facilities from the Philippines, and has been found in pigs in the Philippines.

How is Ebola virus spread?

The first person in an outbreak presumably catches the virus from an animal. After that, the disease spreads primarily through direct contact with the blood and other bodily fluids of an infected person. People can also be exposed to Ebola through contact with contaminated objects, such as needles. In many outbreaks, the disease is spread within hospitals, because in many African hospitals masks, gowns, and gloves are not routinely worn and needles and syringes may be reused.

Can Ebola virus be spread through the air?

Although under research conditions Ebola has shown the ability to spread through airborne particles, there has never been a documented case of a human being infected in this manner in a real-world setting, such as a household or hospital.

Does Ebola hemorrhagic fever cause people's internal organs to "melt" or rot away?

No. However, in severely ill patients near death, internal bleeding can lead to vomiting large amounts of blood, which may give that impression.

Can Ebola virus disease be cured?

No. There is no treatment for the disease at this time. However, supportive therapy, especially fluid replacement, can reduce the death rate.

Is Ebola virus disease always fatal?

No. In the outbreaks to date, the Zaire strain has been the most deadly, killing up to 90 percent of its victims; the second-most common strain, Ebola-Sudan, kills about half of those who contract it. Those who survive take several weeks to recover.

Is Ebola the most dangerous disease ever discovered?

No. Nasty though it is, it is not as contagious as other infectious diseases, such as measles. It is also much more easily contained than viruses such as HIV (which causes AIDS), because people can carry HIV around in their bloodstream for years, potentially infecting other people, before they show any symptoms. By contrast, people with Ebola are only highly infectious for a short period of their illness.

Timeline of Ebola

1976—Strain of Ebola appears in Nzara and Maridi, Sudan, and in the surrounding area. Deaths total 284.
Ebola hemorrhagic fever is named and recognized as a new disease after it surfaces in Yambuku, Zaire. Outbreak kills 318 people.

1979—Ebola-Sudan reappears in Nzara, Sudan, killing thirty-four people.

1989—Monkeys in quarantine facilities in Virginia, Texas, and Pennsylvania begin dying of Ebola. The new strain, which affects monkeys but not humans, is called Ebola-Reston.

1992—Monkeys from the Philippines imported into Sienna, Italy, are found to be infected with Ebola-Reston. No humans are infected.

1994—Richard Preston publishes *The Hot Zone*, which details the outbreak among the monkeys in Reston, Virginia, and raises the possibility that Ebola could produce a horrifying worldwide epidemic.
Outbreak of Ebola-Zaire in gold-mining camps in the rain forest of Gabon kills forty-four people.
A new strain of Ebola surfaces among wild chimpanzees in the Ivory Coast. One scientist becomes ill but recovers. Originally called Ebola-Ivory Coast, the strain is now called Taï Forest.

1995—Second major outbreak of Ebola-Zaire occurs in Kikwit, Democratic Republic of the Congo, and the surrounding area. The disease again spreads through families and hospitals. Death toll is 315.

1996—Ninety-seven people in Gabon die from eating monkeys infected with Ebola.

2000—Outbreak of Ebola-Sudan in Uganda kills 425 people.

2001–2003—Multiple outbreaks of the Zaire virus kill approximately 250 people in the Democratic Republic of the Congo and Gabon.

2004—Russian scientist doing research on Ebola virus dies after she accidentally jabs herself with a contaminated needle.

2007—Outbreak of the Zaire virus in the Democratic Republic of the Congo kills 187 people.
A new strain of Ebola kills thirty-seven people in Bundibugyo District of western Uganda. The strain is named Bundibugyo.

2008—Reston virus surfaces in pigs in the Philippines, the first known occurrence of Ebola-Reston in pigs.

2012—Outbreak of Sudan virus in Uganda kills four, and Bundibugyo virus kills thirteen people in the Democratic Republic of the Congo.

2014—Outbreak in the Democratic Republic of the Congo kills forty-nine people.
First human diagnosed with Ebola in the United States dies. Several people who cared for that patient test positive for Ebola but survive.

2014–2015—A massive outbreak that begins in Gabon kills more than ten thousand people in multiple countries. Gabon, Liberia, and Sierra Leone are hardest hit. Large-scale human trials of two promising Ebola vaccines begin.

CHAPTER NOTES

Chapter 1. Four Decades of Terror

1. Ed Regis, *Virus Ground Zero: Stalking the Killer Viruses With the Centers for Disease Control and Prevention* (New York: Pocket Books, 1996), pp. 107–109.
2. Michael Balter, "Emerging Diseases: On the Trail of Ebola and Marburg Viruses," *Science*, November 3, 2000.
3. "About Ebola Virus Disease." *Centers for Disease Control and Prevention*, accessed March 23, 2015, http://www.cdc.gov/vhf/ebola/about.html.
4. "Transmission," *Centers for Disease Control and Prevention,* accessed March 23, 2015, http://www.cdc.gov/vhf/ebola/transmission/index.html.
5. "Cases of Ebola Diagnosed in the United States," *Centers for Disease Control and Prevention*, accessed March 23, 2015, http://www.cdc.gov/vhf/ebola/outbreaks/2014-west-africa/united-states-imported-case.html.

Chapter 2. Ebola: A Brief History

1. Nancy Emond, "The Plague in Athens During the Pelopennesian War," *The Asclepion*, accessed March 27, 2015, http://www.indiana.edu/~ancmed/plague.htm.
2. P. E. Olson et al., "The Thucydides Syndrome: Ebola Déjà vu? (or Ebola Reemergent?)," *Emerging Infectious Diseases* 2, no. 2 (April-June 1996), Letters.
3. Ibid.
4. Manolis J. Papagrigorakis et al., "DNA Examination of Ancient Dental Pulp Incriminates Typhoid Fever as a Probable Cause of the Plague of Athens," *International Journal of Infectious Diseases* 10, Issue 3 (May 2006),

http://www.ijidonline.com/article/S1201-9712%2805%2900178-5/fulltext.

5. "Outbreaks Chronology: Ebola Virus Disease," *Centers for Disease Control and Prevention*, March 27, 2015, http://www.cdc.gov/vhf/ebola/outbreaks/history/chronology.html.

6. Tara Waterman, "Ebola Zaire Outbreaks," *Tara's Ebola Site* (honors Thesis, Stanford University, 1999), http://www.stanford. edu/group/virus/filo/eboz.html.

7. Ed Regis, *Virus Ground Zero: Stalking the Killer Viruses With the Centers for Disease Control and Prevention* (New York: Pocket Books, 1996), 109.

8. Ellen Wallace, "In His Words: Africa's Deadly Visitor: Terror Imitates Art as the Killer Ebola Virus Makes Another Lethal Appearance." *People Magazine*, May 29, 1995.

9. Sean Henahan, "Dr. Frederick A. Murphy Talks About the Ebola Virus," *Access Excellence*, accessed March 27, 2015, http://www.access excellence.org/WN/NM/interview_murphy.html.

10. Tara Waterman, "Ebola Sudan Outbreaks," *Tara's Ebola Site* (honors thesis, Stanford University, 1999), http://www.stanford. edu/group/virus/filo/ebos.html.

11. "Outbreaks Chronology: Ebola Virus Disease."

12. Waterman, "Ebola Sudan Outbreaks."

13. Tara Waterman. "Ebola Reston Outbreaks," *Tara's Ebola Site* (honors thesis, Stanford University, 1999), http://www.stanford.edu/group/virus/filo/ebor.html.

14. "Review of Human-to-Human Transmission of Ebola Virus," *Centers for Disease Control and Prevention*, accessed March 27, 2015, http://www.cdc.gov/vhf/ebola/transmission/human-transmission.html.

15. Tara Waterman, "Ebola Côte d'Ivoire Outbreaks," *Tara's Ebola Site* (honors thesis, Stanford University, 1999), http://www. stanford.edu/group/virus/filo/eboci.html.

16. Joseph F. Wamala et al., "Ebola Hemorrhagic Fever Associated with Novel Virus Strain, Uganda, 2007–2008," *Emerging Infectious Diseases* 16, no. 7 (July 2010), http://www.ncbi.nlm.nih.gov/pmc/articles/PMC3321896/pdf/09-1525_finalR.pdf.

17. Regis, p. 235.

18. Ibid., pp. 148–149.

19. Ibid., 157–159.

20. Ibid., 149.

21. Ibid., 151.

22. Ibid., 153.

23. "Outbreaks Chronology: Ebola Virus Disease."

24. Ibid.

25. Ibid.

26. Ibid.

27. "Breakthrough on Ebola." *BBC News*, July 31, 2000, http://news.bbc.co.uk/2/hi/health/860319.stm.

28. Stefan Lovgren, and Catherine Roberts, "World: Mysterious Killer: Virus Hunters from Around the World Battle to Contain a Deadly Outbreak of Ebola," *Maclean's*, November 13, 2000, 42.

29. "Outbreak of Ebola Hemorrhagic Fever, Uganda, August 2000–January 2001," *Morbidity and Mortality Weekly Report*, Centers for Disease Control and Prevention, February 9, 2001, http://www.cdc.gov/mmwr/preview/mmwrhtml/mm5005a1.htm.

30. "Outbreaks Chronology: Ebola Virus Disease."

31. Fred Guterl and Shehnaz Suterwalla, "A New Weapon Against Ebola: A Vaccine for Monkeys Holds Out Hope for People," *Newsweek*, November 12, 2000, 91.

32. "Origins of the 2014 Ebola Epidemic," World Health Organization, accessed March 30, 2015, http://www.who.int/csr/disease/ebola/one-year-report/virus-origin/en/.

33. "2014 Ebola Outbreak in West Africa—Case Counts," *Centers for Disease Control and Prevention*, accessed

March 30, 2015, http://www.cdc.gov/vhf/ebola/
outbreaks/2014-west-africa/case-counts.html.

Chapter 3. Anatomy of a Deadly Disease

1. Ed Regis, *Virus Ground Zero: Stalking the Killer Viruses With the Centers for Disease Control and Prevention* (New York: Pocket Books, 1996), 60–61.
2. Mike Bray and Daniel S. Chertow, "Epidemiology and Pathogenesis of Ebola Virus Disease," *UpToDate.com*, accessed March 23, 2015, http://www.uptodate.com/contents/epidemiology-and-pathogenesis-of-ebola-virus-disease.
3. "Patient Information: Ebola (The Basics)," *UpTo Date.com*, accessed March 23, 2015, http://www.uptodate.com/contents/ebola-the-basics.
4. Bray and Chertow.
5. "Transmission," Centers for Disease Control and Prevention, accessed March 30, 2015, http://www.cdc.gov/vhf/ebola/transmission/index.html.
6. "Transmission."
7. "Why Ebola Is Not Likely to Become Airborne," *Centers for Disease Control and Prevention,* accessed March 31, 2015, http://www.cdc.gov/vhf/ebola/pdf/mutations.pdf.
8. Bray and Chertow.
9. Regis, 103.
10. Ibid.
11. Ibid., 104.
12. Ibid.

Chapter 4. Is It Ebola?

1. Ed Regis, *Virus Ground Zero: Stalking the Killer Viruses With the Centers for Disease Control and Prevention* (New York: Pocket Books, 1996), 12–14.
2. Ibid., 18–20.

3. Ibid., 20.

4. Ibid., 21.

5. Ibid, 40-42.

6. "Diagnosis." *Centers for Disease Control and Prevention*, accessed April 1, 2015, http://www.cdc.gov/vhf/ebola/ diagnosis/index.html.

7. Regis, 42–43.

8. Joshua Amupadhi, "Sharp-Witted Doctor Spotted Ebola in South Africa." *Africa News Service*, November 23, 1996.

9. Tanya Lewis, "How Do Doctors Test for Ebola?" *LiveScience.com*, October 3, 2014, http://www.livescience .com/48141-how-doctors-test-for-ebola.html.

Chapter 5. Treating Ebola Virus Disease

1. Laurie Garrett, *The Coming Plague: Newly Emerging Diseases in a World Out of Balance* (New York: MacMillan, 1994), 217-219.

2. "Treatment," *Centers for Disease Control and Prevention*, accessed April 1, 2015, http://www.cdc.gov/vhf/ebola/ treatment/index.html.

3. Yves Guimard et al., "Organization of Patient Care During the Ebola Hemorrhagic Fever Epidemic in Kikwit, Democratic Republic of the Congo, 1995," *The Journal of Infectious Diseases*, February 1999, http://jid. oxfordjournals.org/content/179/Supplement_1/S268.long.

4. Ibid.

5. Dina Fine Maron, "Blood Transfusions from Survivors Best Way to Fight Ebola," *Scientific American*, September 5, 2014, http://www.scientificamerican.com/article/blood-transfusions-from-survivors-best-way-to-fight-ebola/.

6. Declan Butler, "First Trials Of Blood-Based Ebola Therapy Kick Off," *Nature*, December 15, 2014, http://www.nature .com/news/first-trials-of-blood-based-ebola-therapy-kick-off-1.16564.

Chapter 6. Tearing at the Social Fabric

1. Glenn McKenzie, "Terrifying Mystique Surrounds Deadly Ebola Disease in Africa: Some Blame Evil Spirits for Scourge that Kills Up to 80% of Victims," Associated Press via *The Dallas Morning News*, April 10, 1998, 16A.

2. Simon Robinson-Gulu, "Letter From Uganda: A Trip Inside an African Hot Zone. What Happens toa Small Town and its People when the Ebola Virus Erupts?" *Time*, October 30, 2000, 8.

3. McKenzie.

4. "A Return to Kikwit, Zaire—Birthplace of Ebola," *All Things Considered*, National Public Radio, September 2, 1996.

5. Ed Regis, *Virus Ground Zero: Stalking the Killer Viruses with the Centers for Disease Control and Prevention* (New York: Pocket Books, 1996), 153.

6. "A Return to Kikwit, Zaire—Birthplace of Ebola."

7. Ibid.

8. "Ebola Battle Claims a Brave Warrior," *The Toronto Star*, December 18, 2000.

9. "Ebola Kills Dr. Lukwiya," *Africa News Service*, December 6, 2000.

10. "Ebola Kills Nearly 500 Health Care Workers," *NBC News*, January 7, 2015, http://www.nbcnews.com/storyline/ebola-virus-outbreak/ebola-kills-nearly-500-health-care-workers-n281801.

11. "Assessing the Socio-Economic Impacts of Ebola Virus Disease in Guinea, Liberia and Sierra Leone," *United Nations Development Programme*, December 2014, http://www.africa.undp.org/content/dam/rba/docs/Reports/EVD%20Synthesis%20Report%2023Dec2014.pdf.

12. "Ebola Battle Claims A Brave Warrior."

13. Ibid.

14. "A Return to Kikwit, Zaire—Birthplace of Ebola."

15. George Mwangi, "Ebola Survivors Face Fear and Rejection in Uganda," Associated Press via Deseret News, accessed

April 1, 2015, http://www.deseretnews.com/
article/794097/Ebola-survivors-face-fear-and-rejection-in-
Uganda.html.

16. Ibid.

17. Pauline Bax, "Ebola Survivor Shunned as a Zombie Joins
Fight Against Virus," *Bloomberg.com*, July 17, 2014, http://
www.bloomberg.com/news/articles/2014-07-17/ebola-
survivor-shunned-as-a-zombie-joins-fight-against-disease.

18. Leslie Papp, "The Real Outbreak Has Been . . . Hype," *The
Toronto Star*, February 10, 2001.

19. "FACTSHEET: The leading causes of death in Africa,"
Africa Check, accessed April 28, 2015, http://africacheck.
org/factsheets/factsheet-the-leading-causes-of-death-in-
africa/.

20. Papp.

21. Craig Spencer, "Having and Fighting Ebola — Public
Health Lessons from a Clinician Turned Patient," *New
England Journal of Medicine*, March 19, 2015, http://www
.nejm.org/doi/full/10.1056/NEJMp1501355.

22. Ibid.

23. Ibid.

24. "Questions and Answers on Ebola," *Centers for Disease
Control and Prevention*, accessed April 1, 2015, http://
www
.cdc.gov/vhf/ebola/outbreaks/2014-west-africa/qa.html.

25. James Ball, "Ebola Is Highly Contagious . . . Plus Seven
Other Myths About the Virus," *The Guardian*, October 9,
2014, http://www.theguardian.com/commentisfree/2014/
oct/09/ebola-highly-contagious-virus-myths-outbreak-
epidemic.

26. Ibid.

27. Julia Bellez, "Why is Ebola Less Deadly in America than
in Africa?" *Vox.com*, October 28, 2014, http://www.vox
.com/2014/10/24/7059743/why-is-ebola-virus-outbreak-
american-africa-nina-pham.

28. Ball.

29. "Why Ebola is Not Likely to Become Airborne," *Centers for Disease Control and Prevention*, accessed March 31, 2015, http://www.cdc.gov/vhf/ebola/pdf/mutations.pdf.

Chapter 7. Preventative Measures

1. Ed Regis, *Virus Ground Zero: Stalking the Killer Viruses With the Centers for Disease Control and Prevention* (New York: Pocket Books, 1996), 109–110.

2. Ibid., 110–111.

3. "Infection Prevention and Control (IPC) Guidance Summary: Ebola Guidance Package," *World Health Organization*, August 2014, http://apps.who.int/iris/bitstream/10665/131828/1/WHO_EVD_Guidance_IPC_14.1_eng.pdf.

4. Ibid.

5. Eric M. Leroy et al., "Human Ebola Outbreak Resulting from Direct Exposure to Fruit Bats in Luebo, Democratic Republic of Congo, 2007," *Vector-Borne and Zoonotic Diseases*, December 2009, http://online.liebertpub.com/doi/abs/10.1089/vbz.2008.0167.

6. Almudena Marí Saéz et al., "Investigating the Zoonotic Origin of the West African Ebola Epidemic," *EMBOpress*, December 30, 2014, doi:10.15252/emmm.201404792.

7. David Quammen, "Insect Eating Bat May Be Origin of Ebola Outbreak, New Study Suggests," *National Geographic*, December 30, 2014, http://news.nationalgeographic.com/news/2014/12/141230-ebola-virus-origin-insect-bats-meliandou-reservoir-host/.

Chapter 8. Looking to the Future

1. Ed Regis, *Virus Ground Zero: Stalking the Killer Viruses With the Centers for Disease Control and Prevention* (New York: Pocket Books, 1996), 198.

2. Ibid., 200–201.

3. Ibid., 202.

4. Michael Balter, "Emerging Disease: On the Trail of Ebola and Marburg Viruses," *Science*, November 3, 2000, http://www.sciencemag.org/content/290/5493/923.long.

5. Kelly Servick, "What Does Ebola Actually Do?" *Science Magazine*, August 13, 2014, http://news.sciencemag.org/health/2014/08/what-does-ebola-actually-do.

6. Christopher F. Basler et al., "The Ebola Virus Vp35 Protein Functions as a Type I Ifn Antagonist," *Proceedings of the National Academy of Sciences of the United States of America*, August 21, 2000, http://www.pnas.org/content/97/22/12289.full.pdf.

7. Servick.

8. "Categorization And Prioritization of Drugs for Consideration for Testing or Use in Patients Infected with Ebola," *World Health Organization*, February 18, 2015. http://www.who.int/medicines/ebola-treatment/2015-0218_tables_of_ebola_drugs_updated.pdf.

9. Laurie Garrett, "Search for Ebola/From Leafhoppers to Chimps: Key to Viral Outbreak May Be Chain of Transmission," *Minneapolis Star Tribune*, October 9, 1996, 03A.

10. Ibid.

11. "Ebola Test Vaccines Appear Safe in Phase 2 Liberian Clinical Trial," *National Institutes of Health*, March 26, 2015, http://www.nih.gov/news/health/mar2015/niaid-26a.htm.

12. Liat Clark, "Ebola Vaccine Reaches West Africa for Massive Human Trial," *Wired.co.uk*, April 2, 2015, http://www.wired.co.uk/news/archive/2015-04/02/ebola-vaccine-massive-trial.

13. "Ebola Test Vaccines Appear Safe in Phase 2 Liberian Clinical Trial."

14. Clark.

GLOSSARY

antibiotics—Drugs that kill bacteria inside the body.

antibodies—Proteins produced by the immune system in response to an infection.

antiseptic—A substance that prevents or stops the growth of microorganisms.

autopsy—Examination of body organs and tissues after death.

bacteria—A self-contained microscopic organism that eats, excretes, and reproduces—and sometimes causes disease.

biohazard—A biological agent or condition that constitutes a hazard to humans or the environment.

biosafety—Safety with respect to the effects of biological research on humans and the environment.

bodily fluids—Any fluids produced by the body. Blood, sweat, urine, and saliva are examples.

cell—The fundamental unit of all organisms; the smallest structural unit capable of independent functioning.

cell culture—Cells grown in a test tube or other laboratory device for experimental purposes. These cells can be infected with a virus in order to grow more copies of the virus.

chloroquine—A drug used to treat malaria.

cremate—To dispose of a dead body by burning.

deoxyribonucleic acid (DNA)—A substance that encodes genetic information in the nucleus of cells. It determines the structure, function, and behavior of the cell.

diagnosis—The process by which a doctor determines what disease a patient is suffering from.

diarrhea—The frequent evacuation of abnormally liquid feces.

electron microscope—An instrument that focuses a beam of electrons, instead of light, to produce an enlarged image of objects too small to be seen with an ordinary microscope.

ELISA—Enzyme-linked immunosorbent assay. In ELISA tests, a sample of an unknown virus is added to an enzyme that reacts chemically to only one specific virus. In the presence of the right virus, the enzyme turns a specific color.

endothelial cells—Specialized cells that line blood vessels in the body.

epidemiology—The study of epidemics.

euthanize—To kill humanely; to "put to sleep."

feces—The solid waste produced by animals' digestive tracts.

filoviruses—A type of virus that looks like a worm under the electron microscope. The four strains of Ebola and the one known strain of Marburg are the only known species of filoviruses.

gene—The basic unit of heredity; a section of DNA coding for a particular trait.

genome—The complete genetic material of an organism.

immune system—A system of cells that protects a person from bacteria, viruses, toxins, and other foreign substances.

index case—The first person to develop symptoms at the start of an outbreak of disease.

influenza—A respiratory infection, caused by a virus, that can also produce muscle aches, fever, chills, and nausea. Commonly called "the flu."

interferon—A compound produced by the immune system to kill virus-infected cells before they can spew more viruses into the system.

malaria—A tropical disease carried by mosquitoes that causes fever and chills.

microbiologist—A scientist who studies microscopic life forms, such as bacteria and viruses.

mutation—A change in the genetic makeup of an organism.

nonhuman primates—Monkeys and chimpanzees. Humans are also classified as primates.

nosocomial—Originating or taking place in a hospital.

pathogenesis—The origination and development of a disease.

pathology—The study of the changes produced by disease.

placebo—A substance that has no therapeutic effect and is used as a control when testing a new drug.

polymerase chain reaction (PCR)—A method of replicating genetic material.

proteins—The complex type of molecules out of which living tissue is formed.

quarantine—To keep an infected or potentially infected person or animal separate from other people or animals to prevent the possible transmission of disease.

RNA—Ribonucleic acid, the genetic material of the Ebola virus.

shigella—A common African bacteria-caused disease that results in bloody diarrhea.

tissue—A group of similar cells that act together in the performance of a particular function.

virus—An organism that is unable to reproduce on its own. Instead, it invades living cells and tricks them into producing hundreds of new viruses, which spill out when the cell dies and bursts.

FOR MORE INFORMATION

Centers for Disease Control and Prevention (CDC)
cdc.gov
> This is the United States health protection agency, fighting diseases of all types and supporting communities and citizens to do the same.

The World Health Organization (WHO)
who.int
> This is the United Nation's directing and coordinating authority for health, providing leadership on global health matters, providing technical support to countries and monitoring and assessing health trends.

FURTHER READING

Associated Press. *Ebola: From Outbreak to Crisis to Containment.* New York: AP Editions, 2015.

Greenhaven Press, ed., *Do Infectious Diseases Pose a Threat?* San Diego: Greenhaven Press, 2013.

Piot, Peter. *No Time to Lose: A Life in Pursuit of Deadly Viruses.* New York: W.W. Norton & Co., 2012.

Rogers, Kara, ed. *Infectious Diseases.* New York: Rosen, 2011.

Quammen, David. *Ebola: The Natural and Human History of a Deadly Virus.* New York: W.W. Norton & Co., 2014.

INDEX